Birmingham Repertory Theatre Company and Soho Theatre Company present

BEHSHARAM (Shameless)

by **Gurpreet Kaur Bhatti**

First performed at the Soho Theatre and Writers' Centre on 11 October 2001 and then at Birmingham Repertory Theatre from 8 November 2001.

THE**REP**
Birmingham Repertory Theatre

●**soho**
●theatre company

BEHSHARAM
(Shameless)
by **Gurpreet Kaur Bhatti**

Jaspal	Nathalie Armin
Father	Harmage Singh Kalirai
Beji	Shelley King
Sati	Rina Mahoney
Patrick	Johann Myers

There is no interval in this production.

Director	Deborah Bruce
Designer	Liz Cooke
Lighting designer	Jason Taylor
Choreographer	Shobna Gulati
Dialect	Penny Dyer
Stage Manager	Lorraine Tozer
Deputy Stage Manager	Anna Graf
Assistant Stage Manager	Julia Wickham

Set built and painted: Birmingham Repertory Theatre
Sound: Soho Theatre and Birmingham Repertory Theatre
Costumes: Birmingham Repertory Theatre

For Soho Theatre

Press Representation	Angela Dias (020 7478 0142)
Advertising	Haymarket Advertising for Guy Chapman Associates
Graphic Design	Jane Harper
Publicity Photographs	Stuart Colwill

For Birmingham Repertory Theatre

Press Representation	Clare Jepson-Homer (0121 245 2072)
Graphic Design	lpp

Soho Theatre and Writers' Centre
21 Dean Street
London W1D 3NE
Admin: 020 7478 0103
Fax: 020 7287 5061
Box Office: 020 7478 0100
Email: mail@sohotheatre.com
www.sohotheatre.com

Birmingham Repertory Theatre
Broad Street
Birmingham B1 2EP
Admin: 0121 245 2000
Fax: 0121 245 2100
Box Office: 0121 236 4455
www.birmingham-rep.co.uk

THE COMPANY

Cast

Nathalie Armin Jaspal

Trained at Central School of Speech and Drama. Theatre includes: *A Day Like Today* (Young Vic); *Local* (Royal Court); *My Dad's Corner Shop* (Birmingham Rep); *Small Objects of Desire* (Cockpit); *Natural World* (tour). Television includes: *The Jury*, *Deep Secrets* (Granada); *Randall and Hopkirk Deceased*, *Maisie Raine*, *Casualty* (BBC) and *Hands* (ITV). Radio includes: *The Glad House*, *Keep on Running*, *Psyche* (all BBC Radio 4).

Harmage Singh Kalirai Father

Theatre includes: *Arabian Nights* (Young Vic & National Tour); *Bravely Fought the Queen* (Border Crossing); *Riddley Walker*, *The Moonstone* (Royal Exchange, Manchester); *My Beautiful Laundrette* (Sherman, Cardiff); *Dick Whittington* (Grand, Wolverhampton); *The Illusion* (Old Vic); *Passage to India* (Redgrave, Farnham) and *Doolaly Days* (Haymarket, Leicester). Films include: *Guru in Seven* (Balhar); *Brothers in Trouble* (Renegade); *Paper Mask* (Granada); *Partition* (Bandung); *A Very British Coup* (Skreba). Television includes: *The Cops* (World); *Trial and Retribution* (La Plante); *A Touch of Frost* (YTV); *Hearts & Minds*, *Lovejoy* (Witzend); *Medics* (Granada); *The Knock* (Bronson Knight); *The Bill* (Thames); *Family Pride* (Central) and *The Good Guys* (LWT).

Shelley King Beji

Trained: Webber Douglas. Theatre includes: *Ion*, *The Modern Husband*, *Orpheus* (Actors Touring Company); *Tartuffe*, *Women of Troy*, *Little Clay Card* (RNT); *River on Fire* (Kali Theatre); *Macbeth*, *Measure for Measure* (Theatre Unlimited); *Damon Pythias* (Globe); *Danton's Death*, *Heer Ran Jah*, *Troilus and Cressida*, *Antigone* (Tara Arts); *Death and the Maiden* (Wolsey, Ipswich); *Top Girls* (Royal Theatre, Northampton). Television includes: *Angels*, *See How They Run*, *A Secret Slave* (BBC); *Tandoori Nights* (Channel 4).

Rina Mahoney Sati

Rina began acting professionally at just eighteen. Most of her work has been in repertory theatres in the UK, most recently Contact, Birmingham, Nottingham, Oldham and Bolton. She has recorded many plays for Radio 4 and appeared in several 'blink and you miss me' television roles.

Johann Myers Patrick

Born in Nottingham and trained at the Central Junior Television Workshop. Theatre credits include: *Someone Who Will Watch Over Me* (tour) and *Drag On* (Royal Court). Film: *Twentyfourseven*; *The Token King*; *Black Hawk Down*; *Kiss Kiss Bang Bang*; *A Room for Romeo Brass*; *Hei Binders* and *Lava*. Television includes: *The Bill; Casualty* and *Kavanagh QC*.

Company

Gurpreet Kaur Bhatti Writer

Gurpreet writes regularly for *Eastenders* and for *Westway* (BBC World Service). Her half hour film *Dead Meat* was produced by Channel 4 as part of the Dogma TV season. Gurpreet has series ideas in development with Carlton Television and the BBC and is also under commission to Theatre Royal Stratford East. Other credits include *Crossroads* (Carlton) and *Two Old Ladies* (Leicester Haymarket). *Behsharam* was developed on the Birmingham Repertory Theatre Writer's Attachment Scheme and is her first play.

Deborah Bruce Director

Previous productions include: *Oleanna*, *The Glass Menagerie*, *Hello and Goodbye*, *Our Country's Good*, *My Sister in this House* (Theatr Clwyd); *Romeo and Juliet* (Chester Gateway); *The Inheritor* (National Theatre Studio); *Making Noise Quietly* (Oxford Stage Company and Whitehall); *The Woman who Swallowed a Pin* (Southwark Playhouse); *The Asylum Project* (Riverside); *Made of Stone* (Royal Court) and *In Praise of Love* (Theatre Royal, Bath).

Liz Cooke Designer

Recent theatre design includes: *The Magic Toyshop* (Shared Experience); *Les Blancs* (Manchester Royal Exchange); *The Hackney Office* (Druid Theatre Company); *The Daughter-in-Law* (Orange Tree Theatre); *Exposure* (Young Writers' Festival 2000) and *The Glory of Living* (Royal Court); *The Gift* (Birmingham Repertory Theatre and Tricycle Theatre); *Spoonface Steinberg* (New Ambassadors and Kennedy Centre, Washington) and *Volunteers* (Gate Theatre).

Penny Dyer Dialect coach

Long established voice and dialect coach working in theatre, film and television. Recent theatre includes: *Cat on a Hot Tin Roof* (West End); *Redundant* (Royal Court); *The Little Foxes* (Donmar Warehouse); *The Shape of Things* (Almeida); *Buried Alive* (Hampstead) and *The Coming World* (Soho Theatre). Recent films include: Meera Syal's *Anita and Me*; *The Importance of Being Earnest* and *Heaven*. Past includes: *Elizabeth* (film) and *Blue Room* (Donmar Warehouse).

Jason Taylor Lighting Designer
Productions for Soho Theatre Company include: *Office, Kiss Me Like You Mean It, Navy Pier, Stop Kiss, Be My Baby* and *Angels and Saints; Jump Mr Malinoff, Jump; 4 Plays: 4 Weeks; 5 Plays: 4 Weeks* (Pleasance Theatre); *Site Specific; Kindertransport* and *Tulip Futures.* Other designs include 8 seasons at the Open Air Theatre, Regent's Park; *Rosencrantz and Guildenstern are Dead* (Piccadilly); *And Then There Were None* (Duke of York's); 30 productions at Nottingham Playhouse and *The Emaginator,* Trocadero.

Shobna Gulati Choreographer
Shobna has worked extensively as a choreographer and actor in theatre, film and television for the last eleven years. She is very pleased to be working on *Behsharam* (Soho Theatre).

_{THE}REP
Birmingham Repertory Theatre

Birmingham Repertory Theatre is one of Britain's leading national theatre companies. From its base in Birmingham, The REP produces over twenty new productions each year. In October 1999 The REP completed a £7.5 million refurbishment which has transformed the theatre, renewed vital stage equipment, increased access and improved public areas.

The commissioning and production of new work lies at the core of The REP's programme. In 1998 the company launched The Door, a venue dedicated to the production and presentation of new work. This, together with an investment of almost £1 million over four years in commissioning new drama from some of Britain's brightest and best writing talent, gives The REP a unique position in British theatre. Indeed, through the extensive commissioning of new work The REP is providing vital opportunities for the young and emerging writing talent that will lead the way in the theatre of the future. Last season included new plays from Nigel Moffatt (*Musical Youth*), Jonathan Harvey (*Out in the Open*) and Sarah Daniels (*Morning Glory*). This season we look forward to Abi Morgan's *Tender,* and Birmingham-born Gurpreet Kaur Bhatti's first play, *Behsharam* (*Shameless*).

REP productions regularly transfer to London and also tour nationally and internationally. In the last 24 months nine of our productions have been seen in London including *Two Pianos, Four Hands, Baby Doll, My Best Friend, Terracotta, The Gift, The Snowman, A Wedding Story, Out In The Open* and *The Ramayana* at The Royal National Theatre. Our production of *Hamlet* also played in repertoire with *Twelfth Night* on a major UK tour last year and in August played in the grounds of Elsinore Castle, Denmark as part of their annual Shakespeare Festival.

The REP's new Artistic Director, Jonathan Church, joined the company from Hampstead Theatre and his first productions, of Noël Coward's *Private Lives* in repertoire with Patrick Marber's *Closer*, open at The REP in late September.

Theatre for the world. Made in Birmingham.
www.birmingham-rep.co.uk

Artistic Director Jonathan Church
Chief Executive John Stalker
Literary Manager Ben Payne

THE ATTACHMENT SCHEME

Two of the new plays in our Autumn season, *Tender* by Abi Morgan and *Behsharam* by Gurpreet Kaur Bhatti, began life as ideas on our attachment scheme for writers. This scheme was established in 1996 to nurture new plays for Birmingham Repertory Theatre, principally from first-time playwrights. Since then it has developed the work of over 20 playwrights with an increasing emphasis on supporting the work of local writers. The scheme provides them with the chance to research and explore their idea and, if appropriate, work with other professional playwrights, directors, designers, choreographers, actors and other practitioners to maximise its potential. The ultimate aim of the scheme is to provide work for the company to stage. The majority of attached plays go on to be commissioned by the theatre and the majority of these plays go on to receive full productions by the company.

The scheme is financially supported by Channel 4 Television.

Ray Grewal's *My Dad's Corner Shop*

Jess Walter's *Terracotta*

For further information about the scheme please contact:

Ben Payne or Caroline Jester
Literary Department
Birmingham Repertory Theatre
Broad Street
Birmingham B1 2EP
Telephone: 0121 245 2000

Transmissions is The REP's unique project aimed at nurturing the playwrights of the future. It gives twenty-five young people from across the West Midlands region the chance to develop their writing skills in a constructive and creative way. Indeed the wealth and diversity of talent among young writers in the region is becoming increasingly apparent.

Transmissions writers are given the opportunity of working with professional playwrights Noël Greig and Carl Miller to develop initial ideas into full and complete scripts through a series of workshops and constructive feedback.

The scheme also allows participants to meet other young writers in a fun and interactive environment, giving them the support and encouragement needed to expand their interest into an active process with a very definite aim; to see their work performed on stage by professional actors.

In July each year the writers come together with professional directors, actors and designers to present a showcase of their work in the form of the Transmissions Festival. The festival is a celebration and demonstration of their work, enabling them to gain an insight into the collaborative process involved in theatre once the initial writing stage is complete.

This year's Transmissions Festival was another runaway success and has now helped to develop the work of over one hundred young new writers.

"*Transmissions hurtled into its second week, blazing with energy and delivering some of the most provocative and original new work to be seen anywhere in the City.*" Birmingham Post

"*A rich and extraordinary assortment of tomorrow's talent*" Evening Mail

"*It is a brilliant enterprise*" Birmingham Post

THE **REP**
Birmingham Repertory Theatre

If you would like to become involved with Transmissions or want further information about the festival please contact Caroline Jester in the Literary Department at The REP on 0121 245 2000.

● soho
● theatre company

Soho Theatre and Writers' Centre
21 Dean Street, London W1D 3NE
Admin: 020 7287 5060 Fax: 020 7287 5061
Box Office: 020 7478 0100 minicom: 020 7478 0136
www.sohotheatre.com   email: mail@sohotheatre.com   *Gordon's*.

Bars and Restaurant
The main theatre bar is located in Café Lazeez Brasserie on the Ground Floor. The Gordon's® Terrace serves Gordon's® Gin and Tonic and a range of soft drinks and wine. Reservations for the Café Lazeez restaurant can be made on 020 7434 9393.

Free Mailing List: Join our mailing list by contacting the Box Office on 020 7478 0100 or email us at mail@sohotheatre.com for regular online information.

Hiring the theatre: Soho theatre has a range of rooms and spaces for hire. Please contact the theatre managers on 020 7287 5060 or email hires@sohotheatre.com for further details.

Also at Soho Theatre:
16-27 Oct at 9.30pm (not Sun or Mon)
Jenny Éclair in Middle-Aged Bimbo
Radio 4's bit of rough and the only female ever to win the Perrier returns to the West End.

'Comedy heaven .. comedy's panzer-sex-stormtrooper Barbie. Resistance is futile.' *The Herald*

'well written and expertly performed...wonderfully offensive' *The Times*

Soho Theatre Company

SOHO THEATRE DEVELOPMENT

Soho Theatre Company receives core funding from Westminster City Council and London Arts but in order to provide as diverse a programme as possible and expand our audience development and outreach work, we rely upon additional support. Many projects are only made possible by donations from trusts, foundations and individuals and corporate involvement.

THE SOHO THEATRE DEVELOPMENT CAMPAIGN

Soho Theatre Company receives core funding from Westminster City Council and London Arts. However, in order to provide as diverse a programme as possible and expand our audience development and outreach work, we rely upon additional support. Many projects are only made possible by donations from trusts, foundations and individuals and corporate involvement.

All our major sponsors share a common commitment to developing new areas of activity with the arts and with the assistance of Arts and Business New Partners, encouraging a creative partnership with the sponsors and their employees. This translates into special ticket offers, creative writing workshops, innovative PR campaigns and hospitality events.

The **New Voices** annual membership scheme is for people who care about new writing and the future of theatre. There are various levels to suit all – for further information, please visit our website at www.sohotheatre.com/newvoices

Our new **Studio Seats** campaign is to raise money and support for the vital and unique work that goes on behind the scenes at Soho Theatre. Alongside reading and assessing over 2000 scripts a year, we also work intensively with writers through workshops, showcases, writers' discussion nights and rehearsed readings. For only £300 you can take a seat in the Education and Development Studio to support this crucial work.

If you would like to help, or have any questions, please contact the development department on 020 7287 5060 or at development@sohotheatre.com

We are immensely grateful to all of our sponsors and donors for their support and commitment.

PROGRAMME SUPPORTERS

Principal sponsors:

Bloomberg, TBWA\GGT DIRECT and Soho Theatre Company have received an investment from the Arts and Business New Partners scheme to further develop their creative partnership. Arts and Business New Partners is funded by the Arts Council of England and the Department for Culture, Media and Sport.

Performances in the Lorenz Auditorium

Soho Theatre is supported by

First published in 2001 by Oberon Books Ltd.
(incorporating Absolute Classics)
521 Caledonian Road, London N7 9RH
Tel: 020 7607 3637 / Fax: 020 7607 3629
e-mail: oberon.books@btinternet.com

A catalogue record for this book is available from the British
Library.

ISBN: 1 84002 249 3

Cover design: Oberon Books

Cover photograph: Stuart Colwill

Printed in Great Britain by Antony Rowe Ltd, Reading.

Characters

JASPAL

SATI

PATRICK

BEJI

FATHER

for my mother

Thanks to everyone at Soho Theatre
and the Birmingham Rep,
especially to Ben Payne who was
there at the very beginning.

Scene 1

1998. The sound of applause. A room upstairs in a seedy pub/club in a hopeless Birmingham suburb. It is cabaret night. Red velvet curtains are behind a small raised platform on top of which there is an empty microphone.

COMPERE: (*Off.*) Thank you ladies and gentlemen. Remember variety is the spice of life and we've got some red hot vindaloo coming up for you now. Our next act is one of my very own favourites. And she's gorgeous, no really Ladies and Gents, she's…um…she's gorgeous. You'll recognise her from Stars in Their Eyes, where she was pipped at the post by um…by Frankie Goes to Hollywood. (*Bigger voice.*) Coming to you straight from the Handsworth Road, please put your hands together for Kiran Carpenter and her band Asian Invasion!

Sound of applause as JASPAL, a damaged looking Asian woman in her late twenties, comes out wearing a long sequinned fuschia pink dress. Silhouette/shadow of a band. Intro to 'Yesterday Once More' and JASPAL starts to sing with the attitude (though not quite the voice) of a diva. As she approaches the chorus the sound system fails, microphones screech and the singing and the music become inaudible. JASPAL does her best to carry on but to no avail. The audience become unsettled and sounds of booing and hissing start.

(*Off.*) Well ladies and gents we seem to have a few technical hitches. (*Smaller voice.*) Sorry about that love…er why…don't you er…

JASPAL looks pissed off and walks off the stage annoyed.

That's showbusiness folks, up and down quicker than a tart's knickers. We'll have our Kiran back for you in a jiffy. In the meantime, why not make your way to the bar where it's half price for any double with any low calorie mixer. Don't go downstairs!

Scene 2

1998. JASPAL's dressing room. It is a small pokey room with a huge old fashioned dressing table which has three mirrors on it. She is touching up her make up. Knock at the door.

JASPAL: Piss off.

COMPERE: (*Off.*) Someone here to see you love.

JASPAL: Tell them to piss off.

COMPERE: (*Off.*) I'll send her up then.

JASPAL: No. I don't want to see anyone.

A knock at the door.

JASPAL: For fuck's sake.

She gets up quickly, swings around and goes to open the door.

(*Opening door.*) All I want is some peace and quiet.

She is silenced by the sight of SATI at the door. SATI is a young pretty Asian girl, dressed in trendy clothes. She is about twenty. They look at each other for a moment.

SATI: Hello Jaspal. (*Pause.*) Can I come in?

JASPAL moves back as if she is frozen by the sight of her sister. SATI hesitantly enters the room.

You look...nice.

JASPAL stares at her.

You were good. Out there I mean. Shame about the sound...

JASPAL stares.

I like your dress.

JASPAL continues to stare. SATI takes out a packet of cigarettes and lights one up.

Do you want one?

JASPAL: I've stopped.

SATI: What…? Since when?

JASPAL: Since after…never mind. I've stopped.

SATI: Oh.

JASPAL: I didn't know you'd started.

SATI: Oh yeah. It's been a while…not long after…well I started just as you stopped. How about that then?

JASPAL: You shouldn't have.

SATI: What?

JASPAL: Started. I thought you'd know better. Never mind about cancer – they dry out your skin and wrinkle up your eyes and they deplete your vitamin C. You'll have no immune system left.

SATI: So.

JASPAL: So I'd appreciate it if you stopped stinking out my dressing room. Anyway it's no smoking backstage. Fire hazard isn't it. But I don't suppose you thought about that.

SATI: Sorry.

JASPAL: I'm a regular here and I don't need any hassle right. I suggest you take your dirty habit elsewhere.

SATI awkwardly puts the cigarette out. JASPAL goes back to her dressing table and carries on doing her make up.

SATI: Jaspal.

JASPAL: What.

SATI: I don't believe it.

JASPAL: Believe what.

SATI: You've changed. I never thought you'd stop. Not you.

JASPAL: Thought you'd be pleased. You were always on at me.

SATI: I was a kid.

JASPAL: And now you're not a kid.

SATI: No.

JASPAL: That's a shame.

SATI: For who?

JASPAL: For you.

SATI: For fuck's sake Jaspal.

JASPAL: Don't you fucking swear in front of me.

SATI: What?

JASPAL: You heard.

> *Beat.*

Bad habits. You've picked up some bad habits.

SATI: Maybe it runs in the family.

JASPAL: Shut up.

> *JASPAL takes out a can of Red Bull, opens it and takes a long swig.*

You on your own?

SATI: Yeah.

JASPAL: Didn't fancy bringing a friend?

SATI: Not really.

JASPAL: Not even Mr Cardboard.

SATI: Don't be stupid.

JASPAL: I'm not the one who fell in love with him am I?

SATI: I wasn't in love with him.

JASPAL: I see him on the telly. What's his name again?

SATI: Stop it.

JASPAL: I'm only asking. Fuck's sake.

SATI: He's gone. Don't you remember?

JASPAL: Oh yeah. His heart got ripped to shreds. Sorry.

SATI: I was a kid.

JASPAL: So you said.

SATI: I've grown up. I stopped all that a long time ago. Anyway, (*She looks her up and down.*) you're a fine one to talk.

JASPAL: What?

SATI: Look at you. You've turned yourself into her.

JASPAL: I haven't.

SATI: Mummy One's favourite.

JASPAL: This is my job right.

SATI: Being a dead pop star?

JASPAL: It's my living.

SATI: Mummy One would like it.

JASPAL: Shut up about Mummy One.

> *Pause.*

SATI: I saw you on Stars in Their Eyes. You were good.

JASPAL: Was I?

SATI: I felt (*Pause, as she struggles to think.*) proud.

JASPAL: Of what?

SATI: You should have won. You looked great, they did a good job on you didn't they? I mean the hair and the make up and everything…it was all so…believable.

JASPAL: You came to tell me that.

SATI: No.

JASPAL: What do you want?

SATI: Nothing. I don't want anything.

JASPAL: Why did you come here?

SATI: To see you. To see how you are.

JASPAL: After four years.

SATI: Yes.

JASPAL: Four fucking years.

SATI: I know it's a long time, a lot's happened, a lot's changed…

JASPAL: Too fucking right. And don't think you're putting me on any guilt trip. Because I won't have it, right. I won't have it. I've got no bad habits now. No, none. I've read the books, I've done the steps, I've even Feng Shui-ed my flat. I'm me, right, ME.

SATI: Is that why you pretend to be Karen Carpenter?

JASPAL: I told you it's my job, it's entertainment. People like it.

SATI: You look like her.

JASPAL: That's what Matthew Kelly said.

SATI: No, not like Karen, like Mummy One.

JASPAL: Will you stop it?

SATI: Remember that photograph, where she's got that beehive and a handbag the size of a suitcase. What did you call it – the Pakis having the picnic in the park. I wanted to look like her. But it was always you.

JASPAL: Shut up.

SATI: I'm just saying…

JASPAL: I don't give a shit. It doesn't affect me any more you see. Not Mummy One, not Mummy Two, not Dad, not Patrick, not Beji, not you. And if you think you can walk in here and…well you can fuck off…

SATI: I didn't come here to…

JASPAL: I've taken responsibility. I said sorry.

SATI: You didn't.

JASPAL: You walked out and you left me. You left me. You don't know what it was like for me. You turn up here, at one of my performances and expect me to hug you and kiss you and be all happy and excited. Well I'm not. I did everything for you, everything. You never even bothered about me. No-one ever bothered about me except when they wanted to call someone slag or slut or whore or prostitute. I'm dead to you Sati, dead. Look at me, the living dead. Just get out, get the fuck out, I can't stand looking at you any more.

SATI: Don't be like this.

JASPAL: What did you expect?

SATI: I wanted to see you. I wanted us to at least try. I've forgiven you…

JASPAL: Fuck off.

SATI: Don't you think I'm the one who should be angry after all your…

JASPAL: You haven't got a right to be angry, like you haven't got a right to forgive. I protected you from all of it, wrapped you in cotton wool I did. Covered your eyes and your ears and your nose…

SATI: You made it worse.

JASPAL: It was for your own good.

SATI: And you decided that did you, you…

JASPAL: Fuck off. You left me.

SATI: What did you expect?

JASPAL: I waited for you.

SATI: I'm here now.

JASPAL: Get lost.

SATI: Families aren't meant to be like this.

JASPAL: For fuck's sake, I thought you said you'd grown up.

SATI: I'm trying to make things better. For both of us. You're my sister, my only sister, I feel for you, I really feel…

JASPAL lunges at SATI. She takes her face in her hand and holds it hard against the wall.

JASPAL: You feel for me do you? Feel sorry for me do you?

She releases her and SATI half falls to the floor.

You little cunt.

SATI gathers herself together and exits in stunned silence. JASPAL shouts out after her.

That's a shame. Cos I don't feel anything right. I don't feel fucking anything.

JASPAL is left on her own. She calms down and looks around the room. She catches sight of herself in the mirror, then looks towards the door and goes out after her sister.

Scene 3

1994. Day One, The shop. Early evening. The radio is on, 'Wonderwall' by Oasis plays. Half empty boxes of tinned produce adorn the dingy space. There are Boots carrier bags everywhere. SATI, 16, wears an old shalwar kameez and trendy nike trainers. She stands behind the shop counter. She vaguely looks over to the shop entrance and when she feels the coast is more or less clear she begins to construct a kind of love seat next to the counter. She creates the seat out of boxes of tinned beans and spaghetti hoops, a small step ladder and a shop stool. She sprays some body spray on herself. She then takes a deep breath and goes to fetch the pièce de resistance – a life size cardboard cut out of Ian Wright in Arsenal strip. The cut out is bendy and can be manipulated into different positions. SATI sits Ian Wright on the side of the seat closest to the counter, and sits down next to him. She begins.

SATI: Ian, I've thought about what you said and I can't. I mean I don't want to. Please understand. It's not that I don't find you attractive. I do. Really I do. But this isn't about that. I respect you Ian, respect you as a footballer. And everything else about you. I mean you and Debbie, what you have is so great, you've got it all – little Stacey, the house in Surrey, the snooker room, I won't let you throw that away Ian. Of course I love you, I mean I have a love for you. But it's more than a physical thing. We share things together. When you got suspended and missed the Cup Winners' Cup final against Parma - I cried myself to sleep because I felt your pain. Do you understand? Well I'm not like Dani Behr. This is forever, it's not a passing thing. I want us to be like Brian Clough and Peter Taylor. Ian please stop. This has got to be about football, nothing else. Those ninety minutes of epic drama, with heroes, villains, ecstasy and despair. The crowd sings, the players dance…it's a bit like a Bollywood film when you think about it… Have you seen one of those Ian? I'm not changing the subject…I'm just…Ian… Why d'you want to know about them? Alright then. I've got a half-brother, Raju, he's six. And there's my older sister Jaspal, she's the black sheep… Oh, Ian I didn't mean anything by that…Sorry. They say she's the pretty one…I'm not sure who I look like…I think I look like Mummy One, that's my real mum. She's on holiday at the moment, she…

Bell rings to indicate shop door is opening. As she hears the bell, SATI pushes Ian Wright to the floor and scrambles across the love seat regaining her position behind the counter. PATRICK enters. He is a young Jamaican male, carrying a big gym bag.

PATRICK: Alright Sati.

SATI: (*Gathers herself together.*) Oh…hello Patrick.

PATRICK: You on your own?

SATI: Yeah… Uncle Comrade's gone to that new Cash & Carry in Smethwick.

PATRICK: Oh yeah?

SATI: You get a free box of Bangladeshi pineapple chunks when you spend over fifty pounds. He couldn't resist that.

PATRICK: I'll have some gum, oh and some of those jammy dodgers for Jaspal.

SATI: She likes them, says they're good for her munchies.

SATI gets biscuits, serves him, exchange of money etc.

PATRICK: Yeah…er… So you getting on alright here?

SATI: It's okay. Fits in with college. Uncle Comrade's not here much, thank god. He found 2p on the floor the other day. And then he starts having a go at me. (*Mimics.*) 'Pennies make pounds, pounds make tens of pounds, tens of pounds make hundreds of pounds, hundreds of pounds make thousands of pounds and that, beti, is the Retail business.'

PATRICK: How much is he paying?

SATI: Pound an hour. So much for his subscription to Marxism Today. I don't mind, he's alright really. (*Gestures to stock cupboard.*) Beji keeps me company and anyway we need the cash. Hey how's your training? You doing the Ali shuffle yet? (*She does some shadow boxing playfully.*)

PATRICK: Getting there. You know training hard, trying to focus. I'm glad to be out of that office, tell you that for nothing.

SATI: It's good to do what you want.

PATRICK: Yeah man.

SATI: Is everything alright with Jaspal?

PATRICK: She's fine.

SATI: Only the last time I saw her she was a bit low.

PATRICK: You know what she's like. Up and down.

SATI: Tell her we miss her. At least I do.

PATRICK: Right.

SATI: So she's alright?

PATRICK: Yeah, yeah. She's getting used to me being in the flat during the day… (*Suddenly remembering.*) It's Tuesday isn't it, she'll be okay, he always leaves the saag on a Tuesday.

SATI: Dad's speciality. Hey tell Jaspal that Mummy Two keeps trying to fix me up.

PATRICK: Yeah?

SATI: She's a right bloody kuthi [bitch]. I've told her I'm not interested, but she won't listen. She got me to meet this BMW dealer the other week. And when they left us on our own he started crying, he told me he was in love with his brother-in-law. He pleaded with me to refuse him.

PATRICK: What happened?

SATI: I pretended I was deaf and dumb. Any disability you see, puts the family right off. Anyway Mummy Two better watch out, Mummy One will be back soon.

PATRICK: Been gone a while hasn't she.

SATI: Seven years.

PATRICK: Right…er…Oh, before I forget, I saw this (*Hands her a flyer.*) thought you might like to meet Mr Wright for real.

SATI: (*Reads and gasps.*) Ian Wright's coming to Birmingham.

PATRICK: Yeah, opening some clothes shop in the Pallisades.

SATI: (*Slowly.*) He's coming to Birmingham.

PATRICK: You should go, see him in real life.

SATI: Thanks Patrick. This is incredible, it's…

BEJI: (*Shouting, off.*) Sati… Sati…

SATI: Oh god. Beji must have locked herself in the stock cupboard. Give these to Jaspal from me (*Hands PATRICK a box of Milk Tray.*) and tell her I'll come and see her after college.

PATRICK: Take it easy Sati.

PATRICK exits. SATI goes to back of shop, lets BEJI out. They come downstage. BEJI is an old Punjabi woman, she has a permanently miserable expression on her face, but her eyes twinkle. She has a hairy face and no teeth and wears an old punjabi suit, her head is covered with a shawl.

BEJI wobbles slightly, she is tipsy. She speaks with an accent.

BEJI: Where's my tic-tacs?

SATI: (*Sniffs as she hands her the box of tic-tacs.*) How's your friend?

BEJI: What?

SATI: Your friend… Jack Daniels!

BEJI: Behsharam, you know it's for my chest… (*Kindly.*) come on darling let's lock up, I'm tired, that cow Mummy Two's going to bite our heads off.

SATI: It's alright, she said she was taking Raju to Shimla's.

BEJI: Raju is a greedy pig.

SATI: Beji! Besides we have to wait for Uncle Comrade. He is supposed to pay us you know.

BEJI: Take it from the till.

SATI: (*As she locks up.*) We can't, it's stealing.

BEJI: Not stealing, borrowing.

SATI: No. (*Pause.*) Beji.

BEJI: Yes, beta.

SATI: Do I look like Mummy One?

BEJI: Yes beta.

SATI: Mummy One's prettier than Mummy Two isn't she?

BEJI: Yes beta. Anyone's prettier than that old bag.

SATI: Beji!

> *BEJI mutters away to herself and starts to lock up. As she does this SATI picks Ian Wright up from behind the counter and holds him close to her face.*

Sometimes I look at my family and I want to heal the differences. Like you did after you smacked David Howells. Make the peace and get on with the game.

> *She puts him down gently, then turns on a portable TV in the corner of the shop. The voice of Dani Behr comes on, it is The Word. Sati and Beji start to watch.*

Scene 4

1994. Day One, JASPAL and PATRICK's flat. The Carpenters' 'I'm on top of the world, looking down on creation' plays, and transforms into the music on JASPAL's sound system. Very messy bedsit – two chairs and a beanbag in the middle of the room, there is a bathroom area and a kitchen area. The place is dank and the colours are garish and mismatched. It is like no-one has cleared up for three weeks. There is a messy, packed coffee table, covered with tobacco, rizla papers, bits of food, papers, old makeup and empty takeaway containers. JASPAL is partially dressed, having just had sex with Stan, a punter, friend and dealer. A door slams. JASPAL is out of it, she slowly puts her clothes back on and at the same time she smokes the end of an old spliff. Her movements are slow and deliberate. She half sings along to the words of the song. JASPAL starts to build another spliff. She lays out rizla paper and fills it with tobacco. She then opens a small packet, it is the wad of weed Stan has left her. On sight of it she jumps up and goes after him.

JASPAL: Fuck's sake. Come back here you bastard.

He's gone, she picks up a Tupperware container wrapped in a Boots carrier bag which has been left on the doorstep and comes back inside. She puts the container down on the table and walks around agitated.

Fuck's sake. I told him I want an eighth, I told him. Fuck's sake there's hardly anything here. Stan you fucking bastard. Cheapskate. I told him I'm not a fucking slag, this is business. Bastard. I told him, I do it for an eighth.

She picks up a used condom from the floor, she inspects it.

At least he didn't last long. I'll have words with him Karen. Next time.

She throws the condom in a bin. She takes out saag from the tupperware container and tastes it with a spoon.

Oh shit I can't eat this. It tastes of home. I'll have it after, it'll taste like something else then.

She turns her attention to building the spliff.

Oh shit Karen, ganja alert, ganja alert. There's hardly any left. I'll have to smoke it before… Fuck it, he's on the wagon anyway. I'll just make it last.

She joins in the singing of the song which comes to an end.

You might be a skinny bitch Karen, but you know how to carry a tune. Mum would have liked this. She liked entertainment didn't she? She loved you Karen. She'd have been proud of me, if I was a bit more like you.

JASPAL is getting more and more out of it.

Not the, you know, not the dying of anorexia bit though. She'd have been pissed off at that. Mind you, I'm an entertainer as well aren't I? Sort of. You and me Karen, we've got a lot in common. (*She looks down at the floor, its filthy.*) He'll have to hoover this carpet when he gets back. (*She picks up a face mirror, inspecting the areas of dark hair growth.*) Time for beautification Karen. You must have done a bit of that. I bet Richard liked you well groomed didn't he?

She starts applying white bleach cream to her upper lip, so this cream now covers her moustache area. She lies in a star shape in the middle of the stage and continues to smoke her spliff. She hears a door slam, she puts out the spliff, sprays some air freshener, picks up the mirror and viciously starts plucking her eyebrows. PATRICK comes in, puts bag down, goes over to coffee table and dips some roti into the saag. He chews slowly and watches her.

PATRICK: Can't you do that in the bathroom?

JASPAL: Do you want a woman with a thick black line going across her forehead. I don't think so.

PATRICK: I saw Sati, these are from her. (*Hands her the chocolates.*) Said she'll come and see you.

Silence.

JASPAL: What did you tell her?

PATRICK: (*Takes some more food.*) Nothing.

JASPAL: Yeah well, I don't want her getting all upset.

PATRICK: About what?

JASPAL: Anything. She gets upset sometimes. She misses Mummy One.

PATRICK: Sati said she's coming back.

JASPAL: What's it got to do with you?

PATRICK: I'm just telling you what she told me. Jesus Christ Jaspal. (*Pause.*) Do you know how long your mum's been away?

JASPAL: A while.

PATRICK: Seven years.

JASPAL: And?

PATRICK: Don't you think that's a long time for a holiday.

JASPAL: It's not a holiday. It's a religious pilgrimage. It takes that long to do it.

PATRICK: I see.

JASPAL: Fuck's sake Patrick. It's to do with the culture isn't it.

PATRICK: Right.

JASPAL: Aren't you going to ask me if I had a nice day?

PATRICK: I'm the one who's been out all day.

JASPAL: (*Starts taking bleach off with a spatula.*) Oh silly me. Of course. How many people did you beat the shit out of today?

PATRICK: (*Moves away.*) Piss off.

JASPAL: (*Moves towards him.*) No tell me, I'd like to know. Boxing is a science after all. Between Richard and Judy and Countdown, I don't get much intellectual stimulation. Maybe you can provide it. I mean you are the one with the degree aren't you.

PATRICK: This place is a tip.

JASPAL: Though having a degree no longer guarantees one a lifetime of security.

PATRICK: (*Sniffs.*) You need a better quality of air freshener.

JASPAL: Especially if your boyfriend leaves his job and starts dreaming of nights out with Prince Naseem.

PATRICK: This place is a tip.

JASPAL: Sorry mum. (*She relights spliff.*)

PATRICK: You could make an effort.

JASPAL: I'll do it later.

PATRICK: I just saw Stan.

JASPAL: Oh yeah.

PATRICK: Has he been round?

JASPAL: No. Why?

PATRICK: Only asking. So what have you been up to?

JASPAL: Loads of things. I sat here… I watched telly…

PATRICK: (*Starts to tidy up.*) There's nothing stopping you going out you know.

JASPAL: There is.

PATRICK: You could go for a nice walk.

JASPAL: Stop that will you. I said I'd do it later.

PATRICK: Bit of exercise, might clear your head.

JASPAL: I don't need my head cleared.

PATRICK: (*Takes spliff from her.*) Give us a tote.

JASPAL: It's the last bit.

PATRICK: I only want a drag.

JASPAL: I'm trying to make it last.

PATRICK: Who paid for it?

JASPAL: (*Takes spliff back off him.*) And you're meant to be in training.

PATRICK: Who paid for it?

JASPAL: I did with my money actually.

PATRICK: I think you'll find I paid for it.

JASPAL: What fucking difference does it make?

PATRICK: I'm just saying.

JASPAL: Stop going on at me willya. Its not my fault you left your job and we're have to live on the fucking poverty line. What do you want me to say? Two giros are better than one.

PATRICK: Well they are.

JASPAL: Shut up. Stop going on at me.

PATRICK: I'm sorry. (*He goes over to her, puts his arm around her.*)

JASPAL: My head hurts.

PATRICK: I'm sorry.

JASPAL: Why don't you go out for a bit?

PATRICK: For a bit of what.

JASPAL: You could go and see Stan.

PATRICK: I've just got in.

JASPAL: Go on please. Just a five pound draw.

PATRICK: Jaspal.

JASPAL: Please Patrick please. I only need a bit.

PATRICK: You go.

JASPAL: I can't. I've got a period pain.

PATRICK: Thought it was a headache.

JASPAL: It is as well. (*Pause.*) Please Patrick, it'll help me sleep.

PATRICK looks at her, puts his arms around her. They cuddle.

PATRICK: Alright, but I want us to stop. Both of us.

JASPAL: So do I.

PATRICK: Let's make this the last time alright. I need to clean myself up.

JASPAL: So do I.

PATRICK: The last time. Alright?

JASPAL: Thanks.

They carry on cuddling.

So when are you going.

PATRICK: (*Lets go of her.*) For god's sake. I'll go in a bit.

JASPAL: I'm sorry. (*She puts her arms round him.*) I didn't mean it. I'm sorry.

PATRICK: In a bit.

JASPAL: Promise.

PATRICK: I promise.

They hold each other again.

Scene 5

1994. Day Two. The Shop. Afternoon. The FATHER sits on a stool, engrossed in his notebook, he holds a pen. SATI sits on the floor watching TV, fiddling with the remote control. Ian Wright cut-out sits on a chair next to SATI. She watches a Football Focus type programme, which can just about be heard. They both seem to be in their own worlds. The FATHER talks good English, but has a strong Punjabi accent. He wears old trousers, trainers, mismatched shirt and tie and a red tank top.

SATI: Dad it says on Ceefax that Ian Wright dreams of ending his career at Highbury.

FATHER: (*Not listening.*) Oh yes.

SATI: That's good isn't it.

FATHER: Very good.

SATI: It means that the Gunners' strike force will continue to be led by a man who fuses both explosivity and calm in front of the goal; who uses both legs – left and right.

FATHER: Oh yes, I know.

SATI: He's a lethal weapon Dad.

FATHER: (*With a start.*) Where?… Oh yes.

SATI: That rare breed of quick thinkers in the box, always a second faster than any defender.

FATHER: (*Starts to compose a poem.*) Tu… [You…]

SATI: Except most probably Tony Adams.

SATI looks intently at the screen. She shakes her fist at it scornfully.

Forget it Lineker, you're a has-been. Sayonara Gary. Don't you reckon Dad?

FATHER continues to be ignorant of her presence. He continues with the poem.

FATHER: Tu heh… [You are…]

SATI: (*Looks over to cut-out and sings to it.*) Ian Wright, Wright, Wright. Ian Wright, Wright, Wright.

FATHER: Tu heh meri… [You are my…]

SATI: I'm coming to see you Ian. In the flesh. Only two days left.

FATHER: Meri… [My…]

SATI: I'll have to get myself ready. Do all the preparation.

FATHER: Tu meri… [You're my…]

SATI: (*Looking round the shop.*) We'll close early. Uncle Comrade won't mind.

FATHER: Tu meri zindagi meh… [In my life you.]

SATI: I can't wait.

FATHER: (*Looking up.*) Ay. [Came.] Ah yes… (*He puts his notebook down.*) When is Comrade coming?

SATI: After he's finished at the caucus meeting.

FATHER: I need some money.

SATI: Don't we all dad.

FATHER: Can you ask him for me?

SATI: He's your cousin.

FATHER: Yes but he likes you better than he likes me. Always looking down on me because he has this…this shop.

SATI: He doesn't look down on you.

FATHER: (*Looking round.*) What kind of communism is this – where you set up your own small business?

SATI: Leave it will you.

FATHER: Bloody Comrade.

SATI: I'm not asking him.

FATHER: Please.

SATI: No.

FATHER: It's for Raju's tap dancing classes. Mummy Two says he needs private tuition.

SATI: Tap dancing! He already has piano and tennis lessons.

FATHER: I know.

SATI: He's only six.

FATHER: I know. But Mummy Two says he needs it.

SATI: He's your son dad.

FATHER: He's your brother.

SATI: Half brother. I'm not asking Uncle Comrade for anything except my wages.

FATHER: Suit yourself.

SATI: Stop being so immature.

FATHER: Leave me alone please. I have to finish my poem.

SATI: (*Channel hopping with remote control.*) Where is Raju anyway?

FATHER: (*Ignoring her, recites loudly.*) Tu meri zindagi meh ay. [You came into my life.]

SATI: She's probably taken him to the factory with her.

FATHER: (*Starts pacing around the shop.*) Tu meri zindagi meh ay.

SATI: Poor Raju. Amount of sweets she force feeds him, he'll end up looking like one of those leather footballs she makes.

FATHER: Tu meri zindagi meh ay.

SATI: Can't you get past the first line?

FATHER: I'm stuck.

SATI: What?

FATHER: I've got writer's block.

BEJI enters holding lots of Boots' carrier bags.

BEJI: (*Addressing SATI.*) So many special offers. (*She indicates the bags.*) Everything Three for price of Two.

SATI stares at the screen.

BEJI: (*Starts taking makeup out of bags to show SATI.*) I got you special selection. L'Oreal, Rimmel, Maybelline. Red wine spritzer lip liner, ebony and ivory eye pencil and bridal suite blush creme.

SATI: Thankyou Beji.

BEJI: (*Takes SATI's cheek affectionately between her fingers.*) Makeup for day, for evening, for afternoons, for college, for home, for the shop. Anything you want my princess.

SATI: Thanks.

BEJI: Remember is not what you feel like but what you look like. That is the important thing.

SATI: Yes Beji.

BEJI looks disdainfully at Ian Wright.

BEJI: Girls are so beautiful and men are so ugly.

SATI: Yes Beji.

BEJI: (*Looks at FATHER with evil eyes.*) What did he make today?

SATI: (*To FATHER.*) What did you make today?

FATHER: Saag.

SATI: Saag.

BEJI: Did he take some to that girl?

SATI: Did you take some to Jaspal, Dad?

FATHER: Yes.

SATI: Yes.

BEJI: Behsharam. Bucharee. Shameless. Poor girl. Would be better if she died in a car crash.

SATI: Beji, don't…

BEJI: Always doing dirty things with bad men.

SATI: She's not.

BEJI: She used to be such a nice girl, before… Anyway tell him I have some good news beta, letter from Mummy One.

FATHER: Will you please tell her to talk to me? I am her son for god's sake.

SATI: (*To BEJI.*) Dad says will you please talk to him. He is your son for god's…

BEJI: (*Growls with evil eyes at the FATHER.*) Fuck off.

SATI: (*To FATHER.*) She says…

FATHER: Oh for God's sake.

SATI: What does Mummy One say?

BEJI: Sara parvar pyara… [Dear all…] She's having a joyful time.

SATI: Still visiting all the temples.

BEJI: Yes all the gurdwaras.

SATI: Did she say when she'll be back?

BEJI: Soon. She said she'll be back soon.

SATI: Dad, Beji said mum'll be back soon.

BEJI: And we will be one big happy family. Except for Mummy Two and that behsharam kuthi [shameless bitch] Jaspal.

SATI: Mummy One is going to live with us isn't she Dad?

FATHER: Sati…

SATI: You said Dad. Remember you said that divorce doesn't matter. You said it's our culture.

FATHER: Yes beta.

SATI: And now you've got Raju it's alright isn't it?

FATHER: Everything is alright.

SATI: I'm glad. I can't wait to see my mum.

FATHER: Sati you have a new mum now and a brother.

SATI: Mummy Two's not my mum.

FATHER: She is your second mum.

> *BEJI has been observing them. As they have been speaking she has furtively dialled a number on the phone behind the counter.*

BEJI: (*Into phone.*) Everyone hates you, you ugly old bag.

> *FATHER and SATI rush over and father takes the phone off her. SATI leads her away from the phone.*

FATHER: Stop it. I told you before no more. (*Into phone.*) Hello yes. I'm sorry she doesn't mean it.

BEJI: (*Shouts.*) Yes I do. (*Sings.*) Ugly old bag. Ugly old bag.

FATHER: Stop it. (*Into phone.*) Please ignore her. What? Okay. Okay. I see you later.

> *He puts the phone down and rejoins SATI who is now watching the TV. BEJI watches them with evil eyes.*

> She is taking Raju for Chinese.

SATI: Again?

FATHER: (*Stands up and points at BEJI.*) You, I've had enough of you. You are banned from using the phone. Do you understand – banned. (*To SATI.*) Tell her.

SATI: You're banned.

FATHER: And how does she know Mummy Two's mobile number?

SATI: How do you know Mummy Two's...

FATHER: No more of your...your obscene phone calls... My wife and my son. How do you think they feel? I know you don't like them.

BEJI: I don't like them.

FATHER: You never liked me. You're plotting something. I know you.

BEJI: (*To SATI.*) I'm going KFC. You want chicken sandwich?

The FATHER retreats to his seat.

SATI: No thanks.

BEJI: (*Goes out, looks over at the FATHER.*) Now he will start with his rubbish poems.

SATI: Beji, leave him...

The FATHER begins to recite. He does so as if he is in a trance.

FATHER: Mushkal nazar aata tha gala kaught kai marna
Aukhar yai muham bhi teri jambaz nai sir ki.
(*He translates to himself wistfully.*)
It is hard to die by cutting your own throat
Even when you want it, the coward within takes over

SATI: (*She looks over to cut-out.*) Sorry, he gets a bit emotional sometimes...

FATHER: Zindgi sai tau khair shikwa tha
Mudtaun Maut nai bhi tarsaya
(*He translates to himself wistfully.*)
Life is not to one's liking
Yet it takes an age for death to quench the thirst

SATI: Dad, you're depressing Ian.

FATHER: (*Breaking out of trance.*) Where is Comrade?

SATI: I don't know.

FATHER: I'm going.

SATI: Where?

FATHER: To the dole office, to see if they can help me.

SATI: You can't keep going there.

FATHER: I need money.

SATI: For tap dancing lessons?

FATHER: Sati.

SATI: Yes.

FATHER: (*Goes over to her and puts his hand on her shoulder.*) You are a good girl. (*He exits.*)

SATI: (*Gets up and starts tidying all the Boots' carrier bags, addresses cut-out.*) Everyone's got problems Ian, everyone. I mean Mummy Two's not the easiest person to get on with, (*Imitates MUMMY TWO.*) Sati choose a boy before I choose one for you… I mean I don't understand why she's so keen, she's not exactly over the moon being with my dad. (*Pause.*) Poor dad. It must be terrible being hated by your mother. At least my mum doesn't hate me, even if she is off being a pilgrim somewhere. She'll be like you Ian, she'll be our saviour. And we'll all cheer and sing songs when she comes home. Like I did when you won the Golden Boot. Mummy One'll sort Mummy Two out for a start. No more manhunting, no more putting you in the cellar. No more (*Imitates.*) 'educating your daughter is like watering another man's fields.' No more leather factory smells. No more 'Bad girl, sisters are supposed to look after their brothers'. It's not like I'm going to forget.

'Bad girl' by Donna Summer starts playing.

Scene 6

1994. Day three, early evening. JASPAL's flat. JASPAL sits opposite the Ian Wright cut-out. She beholds him suspiciously.

JASPAL: You alright there? (*She waits for him to respond.*) Conversation not your strong point then? (*She gives up on Ian Wright and calls out to SATI who is off-stage making tea.*) Oy, bring them custard creams in will ya?

SATI: (*Off.*) How many sugars?

JASPAL: (*She thinks for a moment before responding.*) Five.

SATI comes in with two mugs of tea and biscuits.

SATI: Bad girl this, bad girl that. Change the record that's what I say.

JASPAL: (*Is building spliff.*) Nothing changes.

SATI: I'm going to meet Ian Wright, no matter what.

JASPAL: Oh good.

SATI: I've planned it all. No-one's going to stop me.

JASPAL: It's good to have a goal.

SATI: I don't care what Mummy Two says, I'm going.

JASPAL: We all need a goal.

SATI: Do you think its because Ian's black?

JASPAL: I expect there is a connection.

SATI: It's not just Mummy Two. It's Dad and Beji as well. They pretend they don't mind Ian but they do. I've heard them say things.

JASPAL: What things?

SATI: About black people.

JASPAL: You shouldn't listen to their shit.

SATI: I don't. (*Pause.*) Sometimes they say things about you.

JASPAL: Really.

SATI: Beji says you go out with a black bastard.

JASPAL laughs as she continues to build spliff.

Why do Indian people hate black people?

JASPAL: I don't know do I? Some black people hate Indians as well y'know…do we have to talk about this. It's so depressing.

SATI: That's your answer to everything.

JASPAL: (*Cheerfully.*) Well I am depressed.

SATI: You want to be depressed more like.

JASPAL: (*Lights spliff.*) I don't.

SATI: Don't lie. Moping about, listening to that sad woman with anorexia.

JASPAL: She has got a fucking name y'know.

SATI: Is it to remind you of Mummy One?

JASPAL: No.

SATI: She was her favourite though wasn't she?

JASPAL: Will you shut up? I'm trying to get off my head here.

SATI: It's not right. (*Whips spliff away from JASPAL and puts it out.*) You shouldn't be doing this all the time.

JASPAL: (*Retrieves it and relights.*) What do you know?

SATI: I know.

JASPAL: You'll understand when you get older.

SATI: That stuff keeps the people down. Robs you of your ambition and self esteem.

JASPAL: (*Smiles as she enjoys her smoke.*) Does it fuck.

SATI: (*Reaches into her bag.*) I've got something for you. (*Hands book over to JASPAL.*) I saw it on Richard and Judy, it's recommended.

JASPAL: (*Reads.*) Healing and Feeling: A Guide to Coping with Addictive Behaviours; An Alcoholic's Perspective.

SATI: Only its not just alcoholics see, it's any addiction. (*Reads from a piece of paper.*) Yes see, it's all of them: drugs, sex, gambling…even biscuits. It's for people who…who've got problems. (*Takes out a tape which she gives to her.*) There's a tape as well.

JASPAL holds book and tape and starts laughing uncontrollably until she falls over and continues to laugh on the floor.

(*Hovers over her.*) Give it a read. You never know.

JASPAL continues to laugh. Eventually subsides.

You've got a lot, Jaspal. You've got this place, (*Looks around – the flat is a tip.*) even though it's a bit messy. You've got Patrick, and I mean, he cares, he really does care. (*Pause.*) Maybe you should make a bit more of an effort, dinner by candlelight or something. I bet he'd love that.

JASPAL: (*Out of it.*) Is there no end to your talents?

SATI: What?

JASPAL: Drugs advice and now relationship counselling. Fucking hell you're only sixteen.

SATI: I'm trying to…

JASPAL: Maybe you should move in. We need some of that round here.

SATI: I didn't mean...

JASPAL: I know, I'm joking. I mean where would we put you… (*Points to cut-out.*) not to mention your famous footballing friend here… (*Pause.*) …do you take him to college?

SATI: Most days, he sort of keeps me company.

JASPAL: Oh yeah, right. Company, yeah. How is college anyway?

SATI: Boring. Full of saddos.

JASPAL: Oy. Don't neglect your education. Education is freedom. That's what dad used to say. Does he still say that? Does he?

SATI: No.

JASPAL: And make some friends will you please? For once it'd be nice if you brought a real life human round instead of… (*Points to Ian Wright.*) …him.

SATI: (*Gets up.*) If you don't want us here we can always…

JASPAL: For fuck's sake, sit down willya…sit down… I'm only having a joke…fuck's sake…why are you so serious …chill out willya, sit down and chill.

SATI sits back down.

JASPAL: That's better. I'm just saying y'know, maybe you should go out y'know with the other students.

SATI: I'm too busy, Uncle Comrade needs me in the shop, and there's Beji to think of.

JASPAL: So she talks about me, does she?

SATI: No… (*Blurts out.*) …well sometimes she says it would be better if you died in a car crash.

Pause. JASPAL laughs.

(*Hurriedly.*) But she doesn't mean it. You know what it's like.

JASPAL: Yeah I know. Dead but with izzat intact.

SATI: I wish they'd let you come home. They might, after all these years. Maybe you could make up. (*Pause.*) Couldn't you say sorry?

JASPAL: For what?

SATI: For all the bad things you did.

JASPAL: What things?

SATI: You know, going out with boys and smoking and all that.

JASPAL: Having a boyfriend isn't a crime Sati.

SATI: I know.

JASPAL: You shouldn't believe their lies.

SATI: I don't.

JASPAL: Do you want to know the real reason I left home?

SATI: What?

JASPAL: I wanted to be a performer. I wanted to be in entertainment. They didn't approve.

SATI: What happened?

JASPAL: I left. That's it. Simple.

SATI: They never said.

JASPAL: They wouldn't would they.

SATI: What about your performing?

JASPAL: I stopped all that ages ago.

SATI: You should start again, do a course or something. You never know, you might become a star one day.

JASPAL: I might.

SATI: And I could come and see you in a show.

JASPAL: Yeah.

SATI: I could bring Mummy One. She'll be home soon.

JASPAL: Who said?

SATI: Beji got a letter from her. (*She recounts.*) She says she's been to all the gurdwaras in India, and once she's done the ones in Pakistan she'll be back.

JASPAL starts building another spliff.

Please don't do that.

JASPAL: Why not?

SATI: Because.

JASPAL: It's my life.

SATI: Can't we be normal and talk?

JASPAL: What the fuck? What's normal?

SATI: Well it changes your state of mind doesn't it – that stuff.

JASPAL: Too fucking right it does – why do you think I smoke the shit.

SATI: I don't think it's very helpful.

JASPAL: Helpful? Helpful? What the fuck do you know? Just shut up willya, you're doing my head in, man. I know I haven't been out much but I think it's still a free fucking country. Shit I can't even enjoy this now, you've done my head in that much.

SATI: That's your answer to everything isn't it, reach for the rizlas.

JASPAL: (*Angry, screams.*) Why don't you shut the fuck up.

Silence. They are both still for a second. JASPAL then continues to roll.

No-one asked you to come round.

SATI: I want you to be alright.

JASPAL: I'm fine Sati, I'm fine.

SATI: No you're not. You look terrible, you never go out and this place is disgusting. You've got to sort yourself out, mum'll be back soon.

JASPAL: She won't be back.

SATI: Don't say that.

JASPAL: Well…the pilgrimage…

SATI: What about it?

JASPAL: She's probably turned all religious fundamentalist hasn't she?

SATI: Of course she'll be back.

JASPAL: Whatever.

SATI: She will. I know she will. (*Pause.*) What's Mummy Two going to do when Mummy One comes back?

JASPAL: How should I know?

SATI: I mean someone has to be in charge. Most probably it'll be mum 'cos she's the first wife.

JASPAL: I suppose.

SATI: My mum's a pilgrim. Like the pilgrim fathers, only she's a pilgrim mother. I could organize a surprise homecoming party for her. Do you think she'll like that?

JASPAL: I don't know.

SATI: Jaspal, do I look like her?

JASPAL: Will you stop asking me all these questions. I don't know right. I can't remember. Leave me alone willya. I just wanted to chill out, have a puff and you're on at me all the time. Stop going on at me.

SATI: Sorry Jaspal.

JASPAL: I've got to go to the toilet.

JASPAL exits leaving SATI alone on the sofa. SATI gets up slowly and gets her things together. As she gets Ian Wright out of his seat, she talks to him.

SATI: It's because I'm a girl. That's one thing I know for certain. I heard them all saying things, I remember hearing the fights. If I'd been a boy dad would never have divorced Mummy One, never married Mummy Two. There would be no Raju. Jaspal most probably would never have got a boyfriend and Mummy One would never have gone to India. If I'd been a boy they'd have had more children – another girl, another boy, another girl, another boy. We'd be like an Indian Brady Bunch. Beji would love dad, dad would be rich and not read poems about dying and I might be an apprentice at Highbury, not just a fan. Jaspal would clean her room and Beji wouldn't drink whisky in Uncle Comrade's stock room. It's an adverse situation Ian. Like when Graham Taylor became England manager. Only there's no-one to sack. Anyway whatever happens, I've got you. I'm going to come and see you at The Pallisades. See you in the flesh. It's going to be a really special day.

Clutching Ian Wright, SATI solemnly turns and leaves the flat. Over to the FATHER who sits in the shop with his notebook. He chews his pen as he contemplates. At the same time, JASPAL comes back in, sits on the sofa and hums in her out of it fashion to The Carpenters' This Masquerade. She smokes the end of a spliff. In the shop the FATHER puts his notebook down, he gets up and recites.

FATHER: I wander'd lonely as a cloud
   That floats on high o'er vales and…
   (*He struggles to remember.*) …something… (*He shakes his head and starts again.*) Ah yes. (He clear his throat.)
   Shall I compare thee to a summer's day?
   Thou art more lovely and more…
   (*He struggles to remember.*) …pretty than….

(He gives up and picks up his notebook. He flicks through it. He sits down. At last he's found what he wants. He looks up and recites.)
Tu meri zindagi meh ay. *(He nods contentedly.)*

PATRICK comes in to the flat.

JASPAL: I feel sick.

PATRICK: What's wrong?

JASPAL: I'm sick.

PATRICK: Don't smoke then.

PATRICK comes and sits beside her and takes the spliff out of her hand and takes a long drag.

JASPAL: Can you not do that please? *(She takes it back.)*

PATRICK: What?

JASPAL: You're meant to have given up.

PATRICK: I'm celebrating. *(He takes it back and finishes it.)*

JASPAL: Don't they teach you about will power in your training. *(She takes it back and tries to take a drag, no joy.)* Oh fuck. Oh fuck Patrick it's dead, its fucking dead.

PATRICK: I thought you were sick.

JASPAL: I am.

PATRICK: I've got good news.

JASPAL: It was only a skinny one as well. Oh fuck. *(She starts looking around for some more, picking up sofa cushions etc.)*

PATRICK: Don't you want to hear it?

JASPAL: There's a blim here somewhere.

PATRICK: Jaspal!

JASPAL: I know there is.

PATRICK gets up and faces her.

PATRICK: I said I've got good news.

JASPAL stops hunting.

JASPAL: Money?

PATRICK: (*Sits down.*) No. Not exactly not yet.

JASPAL: (*Carries on hunting.*) What then?

PATRICK: This American guy's been to see me, they reckon he wants to train me.

JASPAL: What?

PATRICK: He's worked with some of the best boxers in the world, and he wants me to go over there.

JASPAL: But you've got a trainer – Eric or Ernie or whatever his name is.

PATRICK: Eric. Look Eric's not in the same league as this guy. It's a great opportunity.

JASPAL: You're too old.

PATRICK: He doesn't seem to think so.

JASPAL: You're not even that fit. Remember that time we ran for that bus and I beat you.

PATRICK: That was years ago.

JASPAL: You were out of breath in seconds and that was when I had my bad leg.

PATRICK: Can't you be happy for me, for once. It's a great opportunity.

JASPAL: You're living in a dreamworld.

PATRICK: You're a fine one to talk.

JASPAL: Hang on. Hang on let me get this straight. You're going to America? You're going to leave me. You're going away.

PATRICK: I didn't say I was going. I'm saying I've got the opportunity.

JASPAL: So you're not going?

PATRICK: I'm telling you about my day.

JASPAL: For fuck's sake Patrick, for fuck's sake. Are you trying to do my head in or what? If you're not going why bother telling me. I don't care.

PATRICK: I want you to be proud.

JASPAL: What because you like beating people up?

PATRICK: It's not beating them up. It's boxing. I want to box.

JASPAL: But you're wasted. I know I'm wasted. But you, you really are wasted. You had a good job. We had money. I ironed your shirts. We used to have wine.

PATRICK: What are you saying?

JASPAL: Maybe you should go back to work.

PATRICK: What?

JASPAL: Things will get better then.

PATRICK: You don't get it do you?

JASPAL: What don't I get?

PATRICK: I'm doing what I want. For the first time in my life. Don't you understand how important that is. I'm doing what I want. No office politics, no teambuilding, no deadlines, no grey coloured white people sitting opposite me. It's about me for once.

JASPAL: (*Hunting again.*) Where's that blim?

PATRICK: I'm not having it - not sitting in an office day by day, suited and booted having my work checked by a Nicola or a Caroline. (*Mimics.*) 'Your girlfriend rang again, she sounded upset, is she not well?'

JASPAL: It's got to be here.

PATRICK: You've no faith have you.

JASPAL: I'm an atheist.

PATRICK: Not like me. I've always had faith. Faith in lots of things. Father Christmas, Jesus, Allah, Guru Nanak, all them boys. I even thought Muhammed Ali would beat Leon Spinks.

JASPAL: Where is it?

PATRICK: Faith in you and me, even when I had to drag you back home when you were off your face fucking strangers on the streets, I always had faith.

JASPAL: (*Hits him.*) Fuck you.

PATRICK: It's true.

JASPAL: Fuck you.

> *They have a semi fight. JASPAL tries to hit him again. He gets her by the wrists and sits her down.*

PATRICK: Calm down.

JASPAL: Fuck off.

PATRICK: Let's just calm down.

JASPAL: You have to throw that back in my face don't you.

PATRICK: I meant I've always believed.

JASPAL: Every time.

PATRICK: I didn't mean it like that.

JASPAL: Fuck off Patrick. Just fuck off.

PATRICK: I didn't mean it.

JASPAL: Yes you did. Yes you fucking did. I gave up everything for you. I lost my family because of you.

PATRICK: No Jaspal. No. They were gone long before.

JASPAL: I left my family to be with you.

PATRICK: They chucked you out.

JASPAL: They didn't.

PATRICK: Come on you remember…

JASPAL: Stop it.

PATRICK: First your mum went…

JASPAL: Don't you talk about my mum you bastard.

PATRICK: And then you started on that shit.

JASPAL: Shut your mouth.

PATRICK: Fucking those lowlife losers. Your dad and your gran found out…

JASPAL: Shut your fucking mouth.

PATRICK: And then they chucked you out. And I came for you Jaspal. I came for you. Night after night after night.

JASPAL: Who the fuck do you think you are? Jesus Christ, my saviour? Some knight in shining armour, who came to my rescue cos I used to spread my legs for a few quid.

He moves towards the door.

Where are you going?

PATRICK: I need to get out of here.

JASPAL: I want you to call Stan.

PATRICK: Not today.

JASPAL: Please Patrick.

PATRICK: You ask him. I'm sure he'll oblige.

JASPAL: For fuck's sake Patrick. One little fucking thing I ask you.

PATRICK: I'm going out. (*He leaves.*)

JASPAL: Well fuck off then just fuck off. Go to America.
Go with Ernie. (*Pause.*) You don't know what it was like
for me. Or for my mum. You bastard. (*Pause. She calls
after him.*) Remember to ask Stan if you see him.

JASPAL slumps back into the flat. She's anxious and agitated.

Where's that blim?

She continues to hunt frantically.

Scene 7

*1994 Day four, morning. The Shop. The FATHER sits on his stool
with his notebook and pen, trying to compose poetry. BEJI stands at
the counter, she aggressively marks tins of beans with a price gun.
She is deliberately loud, hoping that the noise disturbs the FATHER.
He does his best to ignore her. She finishes all the tins and there is
silence. He puts pen to paper. But immediately stops as she starts
again, making more noise than before. The FATHER's had enough.*

FATHER: Why are you doing this?

BEJI: I'm a worker. I have to work.

FATHER: You are doing it on purpose. To disturb me.

BEJI: Comrade told me to put the prices…

FATHER: Why do you torture me like this?

BEJI: Comrade is my manager. I have to do my work.

FATHER: Bloody Comrade.

> *BEJI carries on doing the prices.*

You should be on my side.

> *BEJI carries on doing the prices.*

I am your son. Your only son.

> *BEJI carries on doing the prices.*

Please stop that noise.

She carries on.

Please stop it.

She carries on.

I said stop.

He gets up, grabs the gun out of her hands and throws it against the wall. It breaks. They are silent for a moment. BEJI starts to laugh.

What's so funny?

BEJI: You broke it. You will have to pay Comrade.

FATHER: I won't.

BEJI: I'll tell Comrade. He will make you.

FATHER: No he won't. He likes me. He helps me…

BEJI: He helps you because he likes your new wife. He likes Mummy Two.

FATHER: Shut up.

BEJI: He likes to do things to her.

FATHER: Stop lying.

BEJI: I have seen them.

FATHER: I'm not listening to you.

BEJI: Who can blame her? With you as a husband, who can blame her?

FATHER: Leave me alone.

BEJI: Comrade gives you money and Mummy Two pays him back with her fat body.

FATHER: Why do you hate me so much?

BEJI: Why are you so useless? Always going to the dole office, always asking Comrade for money. What sort of man loses control of his family like this?

FATHER: I do my best.

BEJI: And Raju, what about him? Mummy Two is always overfeeding him, making him do piano lessons and tap dancing.

FATHER: He likes it.

BEJI: Your son is turning into your daughter.

FATHER: Shut up.

BEJI: You let her spoil him, she spends too much money. I wish you'd never brought her here.

FATHER: Mummy Two is my wife. The mother of my son, she…

BEJI: And what about Mummy One?

FATHER: It was your fault, you were supposed to look after her.

BEJI: Don't you talk to me like that you bastard, she was your wife. She was your responsibility.

FATHER: Leave me alone.

BEJI: She was weak, she needed you.

FATHER: I'm not listening.

BEJI: You should have kept her. Kept both of them. Mummy One and Mummy Two.

FATHER: I did my best.

BEJI: You have no backbone. Is this what I gave birth to? A spineless weak tosser?

FATHER: No-one ever gave me a chance. And you, you were always there waiting for it to go wrong.

BEJI: Sati is beginning to ask questions. She wants to know.

FATHER: Don't you tell her anything.

BEJI: I'm not going to tell, you bastard. I'm not as stupid as you.

FATHER: Why are you doing this?

BEJI: Sati goes to see that behsharam Jaspal. What if she tells her? Then what will you do?

FATHER: She is a drug addict, she doesn't remember.

BEJI: How do you know?

FATHER: I know.

BEJI: Jaspal brought so much shame on us and you did nothing.

FATHER: What did you want me to do? Kill her?

BEJI: You couldn't kill a fly. You're too bloody useless.

FATHER: Leave me alone, I'm trying to write my poem.

The FATHER turns his attention to his notebook again. Beji goes and retrieves the price gun, she starts the pricing again. Qawaali music starts to play.

BEJI: What about Sati? Always sitting with that black cardboard man, talking to him. It's not normal.

FATHER: Shut up, she will hear you.

BEJI: And what if she becomes like Jaspal? What will you do then?

FATHER: Sati is a good girl.

BEJI: You make me sick. You and your poems. What kind of man are you?

Qawaali music plays louder, as the emotion approaches crescendo, it gets bigger and bigger and ends in a deafening scream. Silence. The FATHER and BEJI look up at the same time, as though something terrible has happened. They then look down again and carry on with what they were doing. SATI comes running in from the stock room. In one hand she holds the head of Ian Wright, in the other the rest of his body from the cardboard cutout. Someone has cut Ian Wright's head off.

SATI: Look what she's done!

FATHER: (*Briefly distracted from the book.*) What happened?

SATI: Mummy Two…she's cut his head off.

FATHER and BEJI are unmoved by this, they carry on with what they are doing.

BEJI: Sit down beta.

SATI: No I won't. I'm sick of this. Sick of her always looking through my stuff, saying this and that, saying I'm bad like Jaspal, not letting me go out, telling me to get married…

BEJI: We not get married. We're not getting you married. Men are all dogs…I've heard about those women…you know…there are those women who don't need men, you will be like them, you will be a lesbian. With the lipstick.

SATI: No, you don't understand.

BEJI: You can still have children, they put it in the fridge.

SATI: NO. (*To FATHER.*) You've got to tell her dad. Tell her off, make her stay away from my stuff.

FATHER: What can I do?

SATI: You're my dad.

FATHER: It's not my fault.

SATI: Dad, tell her…

FATHER: Please listen to Mummy Two.

BEJI: Sit down beta. (*Points to telly.*) Fast Show is coming soon.

SATI: NO. Dad I need you to help me, to back me for once. I'm your daughter. Please.

FATHER: I can't do anything.

SATI: Please dad.

FATHER: It's not my fault.

SATI: I want my mum.

FATHER: Don't blame me.

SATI: I want my mum. I want her.

BEJI: She's coming back soon beta.

SATI: When? You keep saying that, but she never comes does she? Does she dad?

FATHER: It was not Mummy Two who cut his head off, it was her. (*Points to BEJI.*)

BEJI: Kutha, haramzada. Bloody liar, bloody liar. You dog, you bastard, bloody liar.

FATHER: It was her, I saw her cut it.

BEJI grabs the phone and dials. FATHER rushes over to her.

No more, no more phone calls, I told you.

BEJI: (*Into phone.*) Next time we'll cut your head off. You bloody cow.

FATHER: Stop it. Stop it. (*He grabs the phone off her, tries to speak to MUMMY TWO, she has hung up. To BEJI.*) Go to hell. Just go to hell.

BEJI: I am already in it.

FATHER: (*To SATI.*) It was her, I saw her cut it. She got drunk and then she did it. She's always drunk.

SATI: Dad, stop making things up. She's your wife, you've got to deal with her.

FATHER: It's not my fault.

BEJI: (*To SATI.*) No backbone, he has no backbone. He is a tosser.

FATHER: You call me a tosser.

BEJI: Always writing his rubbish poems.

FATHER: I need to express myself, no-one here listens to me.

BEJI: Rubbish poems.

FATHER: (*To BEJI.*) You are jealous, you have always been jealous of me.

SATI: Dad, you're not listening, Mummy Two's…

FATHER: Mummy Two what? Mummy Two what? She is not your enemy. All my life I have done everything for you people. So that you would have a mother.

SATI: I've already got a mother.

FATHER: I can't listen any more. No more. All of you against me.

SATI: Dad.

FATHER: I'm tired of this. Tired of waiting for Comrade. I'm going.

SATI: Dad!

FATHER: I have to go.

FATHER exits taking his book with him. There is a pause in the action. BEJI produces another Boots' bag, and takes a card out of it.

BEJI: Look beta, postcard from your mum, from a new Gurdwara in Pakistan.

SATI: Well she's not here is she? She's not here.

SATI moves away from BEJI with the head and body of cardboard cut-out. Lights dim on BEJI although her silhouette can still be seen. Light on SATI at the side of the stage. She is still upset, pulls herself together and manages to talk to Ian Wright.

(*To cut-out.*) I'll put you back together. Don't worry. Cutting you up in pieces, it's not fair, not right. I'll be seeing you soon anyway, (*Checks watch.*) in a few hours. (*Pause.*) I love you Ian Wright (*Kisses the face passionately.*) I swear that's the God's honest truth. Whatever they say, they can't take you away from me.

SATI exits.

Scene 8

1994. Day four, afternoon. JASPAL lies down alone, she is partially dressed, having just had sex with Stan again. She gets up and slowly puts her clothes back on and at the same time she smokes a spliff. She is out of it.

JASPAL: (*Half singing/half speaking.*) In your mind you have capacities to know. To telepath messages through the vast unknown. (*She picks up two used condoms from the floor, she wanders across the room and throws them in the bin.*) Please close your eyes and concentrate on every thought you think. Upon the recitation we're about to say. Calling occupants of interplanetary craft. Calling occupants of interplanetary craft. Poor little Karen. Poor Mummy One. Calling occupants of interplanetary, most extraordinary craft. (*As if in a trance. She is out of it, she takes a long drag and walks about shakily.*) Please interstellar policeman. Won't you give us a sign. Give us a sign. Alright Mum. It's alright. I'm coming now. (*She looks up and her look changes to one of horror.*) Oh no. (*She puts a hand between her legs.*) Mum…Mum…you silly, bad… You're not meant to do that. Oh no. It's beginning to bleed. Oh, fuck, fuck…It's all on me. You've got it all on me. No, there's no thing inside. There's nothing. You messy, bad, dirty thing. (*She sits down.*) I'll do it. I said I'll do it. Bad bloody messy Mum. (*Half singing.*) Please interstellar policeman won't you give us a sign that we've reached you. Poor little thing. What a shame. Poor little Mummy Karen. Bye Mum. Bye. (*She waves out to the audience.*) Say bye to Mummy, Sati, say bye. Good girl. (*Motherly*) Come and sit down. Do you want some fish fingers? Poor little Sati, Mummy Karen. (*Half singing.*) We are your friends. Poor bad Mummy One. Poor Jaspal. Bad bloody messy girl. Dirty whore. Sucking men on the streets. Fucking black men for a bit of black. (*Half singing.*) Calling occupants of interplanetary craft. We are your friends.

She gets under a cover and lies down. PATRICK comes in. He puts his bag down and goes to get a drink.

PATRICK: Jaspal, it's the middle of the afternoon.

No response.

Come on you can't stay in bed all day.

JASPAL: No.

PATRICK: You've got to get up sometime.

JASPAL: I know.

PATRICK changes his clothes.

PATRICK: What's wrong with you?

JASPAL: I'm not well.

PATRICK: You're never well.

JASPAL: I miss my mum.

PATRICK comes over and sits by her.

PATRICK: Why don't you try getting in contact with her?

JASPAL: I can't.

PATRICK: Why not? Ask Sati to ask your dad.

JASPAL: I can't.

PATRICK: She writes to them doesn't she?

65

JASPAL: Yeah.

PATRICK: Then ask.

JASPAL: No.

PATRICK: For god's sake Jaspal.

JASPAL: What?

PATRICK: You've got to want to help yourself.

No response.

We need to talk.

JASPAL: We are.

PATRICK: I mean like adults. Like other people do. You know, they weigh things up, consider the options and decide on an outcome.

JASPAL: What?

PATRICK: I want to talk about America.

JASPAL: America?

PATRICK: Yes.

JASPAL: Why?

PATRICK: I want us to think about going.

JASPAL: It's your life.

PATRICK: It's not.

JASPAL: It is. It so is your life.

PATRICK: It's our life.

JASPAL: I can't.

PATRICK: Why?

JASPAL: I just can't.

PATRICK: But...

JASPAL: Don't Patrick, please don't. Leave me if that's what you want, leave me and go and live with Eric and Ernie in America, but don't ask me…because…I can't…I can't think…about anything…

PATRICK: I didn't say I want to leave you.

JASPAL: Stop please…My head's full as it is. Leave me alone.

PATRICK: (*Looking round.*) Has Stan been here?

JASPAL: What?

PATRICK: Has Stan been here?

JASPAL: No.

PATRICK: (*Picks up tobacco tin.*) What's his tin doing here then?

JASPAL: He lent it me. The other week.

PATRICK: Don't lie.

JASPAL: I'm not. Patrick. Fuck's sake.

PATRICK: You've been fuckin' him haven't you?

JASPAL: What? I haven't.

PATRICK: Don't lie, you have haven't you…you bitch, you fucking bitch.

JASPAL: I haven't. I swear I haven't.

PATRICK: Where's that weed come from then?

JASPAL: It's mine, I found it. I've had it ages…Patrick… Please…

PATRICK: You don't care do you, you don't care about anyone else.

JASPAL: I do. I do care…please stop it. I haven't done anything.

PATRICK: What kind of man do you think I am?

JASPAL: A nice one. Please stop shouting…Please…I haven't done anything wrong…

PATRICK: What the fuck am I doing here?

JASPAL: I'm not well…You know what I'm like. I can't help it…you know…my head's full as it is…

JASPAL crumbles on a chair. PATRICK comes right up to her. She tries to move away.

PATRICK: What about me? What about me Jaspal? Have you for one minute ever thought about me? Don't you think my head's full? People have been filling it since I first laid eyes on you.

JASPAL: Go away.

PATRICK: (*Plays his mother, an older Jamaican woman.*) She's a pretty girl, you know your grandmother was Indian. You love her, she love you, don't you pay no mind to her family. Ah the grandchildren will be so beautiful. Hear now, she the same colour as you, one shade lighter maybe, we all the same underneath.

He moves right up to her face, she tries to move away, she can't.

JASPAL: Stop it.

PATRICK: (*Plays his friend Carlton.*) Yeah man, asian girls, boy I'm tellling you, I like a bit of Indian now and again. It's just like the Irish girls at school, they ain't allowed to have it, and when they get it boy – they go like the clappers. They're different P, like the girls in Hawaii Five O used to be, well exotic – that skin, those eyes, that hair. Everyone wants an Asian babe on their arm. You seen that magazine, Raas claat! (*Plays his friend Joe, a rastafarian.*) Why you want to pollute your race, man? You is a black man, try fuckin' a black woman.

JASPAL: Stop.

PATRICK: (*His mother.*) Patrick, I seen her walking the streets with the next man. She selling her body. Oh god, my son, my son, get rid of that slut. She no good.

JASPAL: Stop will you, please.

PATRICK: (*Joe.*) These Pakis man, they look down on us, look at the way she's carrying on. Problems we all got problems, where's your self respect. (*Carlton.*) Alright man, so she's sorted herself out, she likes her weed though don't she, she don't do nothing all day, that's rubbish man.

JASPAL: Get away from me.

She tries to move away, he follows her round the room.

PATRICK: (*Mother.*) Leave her, please, son, she's a nice girl, but she's ill, you can do better than that. (*Joe.*) Why you want to pollute your race? (*Carlton.*) You like her don't you. You like that whore.

JASPAL starts to cry, she falls to the floor. Patrick moves away from her.

JASPAL: Stop, just stop.

PATRICK: I'm going out. (*Begins to exit.*)

JASPAL: Patrick…Patrick…I'll stop. I'll be good. I will. I'll change, I will, I promise.

Silence.

Where are you going?

PATRICK: To sign on.

JASPAL: Please… (*She clambers after him.*)

PATRICK: Get away from me.

PATRICK picks up his bag and slowly walks out of the flat, past a distraught JASPAL.

JASPAL: Please don't leave me like this...Patrick... (*She clambers back to the refuge of her seat.*) Don't leave me like this. Not all cut up like this. It hurts. (*She puts her hands between her legs.*) Help me, please God, help me. (*She sits rocking. She looks around her, she is distressed. She catches sight of the book which SATI bought her. She breathes deeply and goes to pick it up.*)

Scene 9

1994. Day four, afternoon. The dole office. The FATHER is sitting down with his poetry book. PATRICK enters, takes a ticket, and sits down, he does not notice the Father. PATRICK takes out a book about Muhammed Ali, and starts to read. The FATHER watches him and moves his hand to the inside of his jacket pocket as though he is checking his wallet. He looks at PATRICK more intently and notices the book PATRICK is reading.

The number machine, which indicates whose turn it is, flicks over to the next number. Both men look at their tickets and then go back to their books. FATHER keeps looking at PATRICK. PATRICK does not acknowledge the looks.

FATHER: (*Brightly.*) Too long to wait.

PATRICK looks up briefly. He does not know who the FATHER is and the FATHER does not know who PATRICK is. However, for a split second PATRICK experiences a moment of recognition, which he can't quite work out. It is enough to make him slightly wary at the start of the scene. He nods politely at the FATHER and then looks back down at his book. The FATHER is glad for this acknowledgement and sees it as a way in to talking to PATRICK. Father moves a seat closer to PATRICK.

(*Indicates PATRICK's book.*) The best.

PATRICK half smiles and nods again.

The greatest.

PATRICK: No question.

FATHER: The Rumble in the Jungle is my favourite.

PATRICK: Yeah it's a popular one I…

FATHER: The fight of the century.

PATRICK: So they say.

FATHER: (*Points to cover photo of Muhammed Ali.*) I am fan…

PATRICK: Right.

FATHER: You too are…interested…

PATRICK: I am…well I box, I'm a boxer.

FATHER: (*Now delighted, moves closer, loosens tie, takes off glasses.*) Oh, that is wonderful, wonderful, you are real boxer.

PATRICK: I mean I'm hoping to turn professional, maybe try my luck in America…

FATHER: America! America! Very good, very nice. Maybe you will meet the…erm…what is his name…the… Angelo Dundee… He is very nice, I like him.

PATRICK: We'll see.

FATHER: America. Yes, America is very nice, but also the society is very consumerist.

PATRICK: Yes it is.

FATHER: You are real boxer. I think you will be lucky.

PATRICK: I hope so.

FATHER: No hoping, do not hope, you must believe, be clever, quick off the mark, one step ahead. (*He smiles at PATRICK like a child and slowly throws some punches in the air.*)

PATRICK: That's right.

FATHER: One step ahead like him. (*Indicates photo of Muhammed Ali on book.*) I remember Zaire 1974 – Muhammed was representing the grace, the beauty and the skill, and George was representing the brutality and the destruction. Everybody in the world thought Muhammed would lose, and even that George might kill him, everybody except ME. I knew that he was too clever you see, too clever for George. All us people, all my Pakistani friends, all of us we used to recite poetry together, he was ours, our hero. Funny if you think, so many of my people all round the country getting together to watch two (*Hesitates.*) of your people fight a boxing match.

PATRICK: Well that's sport for you, bringing people together.

FATHER: And also dividing people. My son he supports Arsenal, he meet a girl from Tottenham, he say (*Overacts.*) I hate her, I hate her. She is rubbish. (*Pause.*) So the sport is also dividing people.

PATRICK: Yes.

FATHER: (*Comparing hands.*) But we, we are nearly same colour.

PATRICK: Yes.

FATHER: Nearly same colour, but totally different culture. (*He laughs.*)

Number machine changes.

FATHER: Too much time.

PATRICK: Yeah.

FATHER: I like people. All people. Not backward like some. Some people from villages, our villages in India you know they have no sense. I am not like that. (*Pause. Quietly.*) I am a poet.

PATRICK: Really.

FATHER: (*Points to photo of Muhammed Ali.*) Like Muhammed. (*Eagerly.*) You know – Me. We. You must have heard of it.

PATRICK: Yes I think…

FATHER: He is professor of poetry at Oxford University. Honorary. You should know these things. You must know. You are a boxer.

PATRICK: Well if you…

Number machine changes.

FATHER: I feel so shame. So much shame. To come here, get Unemployment Benefit.

PATRICK: One of those things.

FATHER: Only temporary measure. I am waiting for new book to be published. Poetry. My wife gone abroad on business, so I must come here. Only temporary measure.

PATRICK: I understand. (*Pause.*) For me too, till it all takes off. (*Boxes playfully.*) You know.

They laugh.

FATHER: I know, yes. You have not got wife.

PATRICK: Girlfriend.

FATHER: (*Laughs playfully.*) Girlfriend.

PATRICK: (*Laughs with him.*) Yes.

FATHER: She love you?

PATRICK: Well it's difficult…

FATHER: (*Laughs.*) Yes, I know it.

PATRICK: It's difficult.

FATHER: And you love her.

PATRICK: In a way I…

FATHER: So why not marry.

PATRICK: Well…

FATHER: (*Interrupts.*) She no work?

PATRICK: No.

FATHER: Maybe it is better.

PATRICK: She has a few problems, you know how some families are.

FATHER: Oh yes. I know, I know very well. I feel sorry for them.

PATRICK: Who?

FATHER: The people with the bad families. It is not their fault, they are not educated. Now me, I like the education. For girls as well. My one daughter, she is scientist, doing PhD, gone away to study. My son he will be physiotherapist, he like sports you know. And my other son, well he will be businessman.

PATRICK: That's good.

FATHER: Very good.

PATRICK: So you don't need to worry about them.

FATHER: No. No way. I'm really quite a lucky fellow. Good work. Good family, everything good.

A beat.

Very quiet here today.

PATRICK: Yes.

FATHER: Peaceful… Sometimes it is so busy at home. There is no peace.

PATRICK: I know what you mean.

FATHER: Yes. I know you know. I know you are very clever.

They laugh jovially.

PATRICK: Thank you.

FATHER: (*Waves hand at him.*) No need to thank… Sometimes I come here just to think and to write my poems. Sometimes even when I do not have to sign on.

PATRICK: Really?

FATHER: Yes… It is quiet usually.

PATRICK: Usually.

FATHER: Except when there is a rumpus.

PATRICK: Yes.

FATHER: You would like to hear a poem?

PATRICK: Yes. Yes why not?

FATHER: (*Clears his throat.*) Tu meri zindagi meh ay.

Pause.

PATRICK: That's lovely.

FATHER: It is not finished yet.

PATRICK: Oh I'm sorry, please…carry on.

FATHER: I can't. I have writer's block.

PATRICK: What does it mean?

FATHER: What?

PATRICK: What you just said.

FATHER: Tu meri zindagi meh ay… You came into my life…

PATRICK: You came into my life… (*He starts thinking.*) You came into my life… And I decided to make you my wife! How about that?

FATHER: No. You are boxer, I am poet. It is better this way.

Number machine changes. They continue to wait.

Scene 10

1994. The stage is divided into two areas: JASPAL's flat and a section of Uncle Comrade's Shop. JASPAL sits reading the book SATI left for her: Healing and Feeling: A Guide to Coping with Addictive Behaviours; An Alcoholic's Perspective. She gets up with a start and madly searches for a pen and notepad which she finds under a pile of rubbish. She returns to the book. She has the book in one hand, pen in the other and notepad on her lap. She reads carefully and thoroughly as though she is studying a list.

JASPAL: Yes. (*As though she is answering a question. Ticks notepad. Reads.*) Yes. (*Unsure. Ticks notepad. Reads.*) Yes (*Definite. Ticks notepad. Reads.*) Yeees. (*Anxious. Ticks notepad. Reads.*) Um. Not sure. Yes. (*Embarrassed. Ticks notepad. Reads.*) Yes (*Quickly. Ticks notepad. Reads.*) Yes. (*Quickly. Ticks notepad. Reads.*) Yes. (*Quickly. Ticks notepad. Reads.*) YES (*Shouts. Ticks notepad. Reads.*) Yes. (*Fearful. Ticks notepad. She puts the tape in a tape recorder. It starts to play. The voice is a long Californian drawl.*)

VOICE: (*From cassette.*) Six or more *yes*es: shit, you have serious addictive tendencies. You could be a risk to yourself as well as others. You need professional help NOW. Please seek it for your own sake. Or you can simply carry on listening. Change your life, save yourself today!

Doing this exercise has made JASPAL confused and horrified. She looks around her.

JASPAL: (*Under her breath.*) Carry on.

SATI enters the section of Uncle Comrade's shop with Ian Wright cut-out. She grabs some sellotape and sticks his head back on. She stands the mended cut-out on one side. She is still in her shalwar kameez, she looks over at Ian Wright and in a coy fashion takes her kameez off to reveal a JVC shirt with number 8 and legend written on the back. She puts a tape in an old cassette recorder and holds the cut-out close to her as though they are poised to start dancing.

JASPAL continues to listen to the tape.

VOICE: (*From cassette.*) This is your moment. You have the power. You have the control. You know what.

JASPAL: What?

VOICE: (*From cassette.*) Look around you.

JASPAL looks around the flat.

Do you see unmanageability?

She nods.

Do you feel it deep down inside of you?

JASPAL: I think so.

VOICE: (*From cassette.*) You've got to get rid of it. You've got to let it go. But first, you have to let yourself feel. Feel all those feelings. Once you do that you'll be free. Doesn't that sound good?

JASPAL: Yes.

VOICE: (*From cassette.*) Think about it, think about how special it could be. How wonderful and perfect. That moment of freedom you've been waiting for all your life.

In the shop 'Chura Liya' ['Stolen'], a famous Hindi love song plays. SATI begins a love dance which she does with Ian Wright. She mimes the words to the song.

SATI: Chura Liya he tum ne jo dil ko. [You've stolen my heart.]

SATI and Ian Wright dance together. JASPAL now has her eyes closed and is relaxed.

VOICE: (*From cassette.*) How good does that feel? Now first lets look at that virus which has been attacking your soul.

JASPAL opens her eyes and looks worried.

77

Yes that's right its fear. F. E. A. R. Fear. Get it out of your system, out of your body, wash it right out of your hair. Do you want to (*Spells out letters.*) F. E. A. R. Fuck Everything And Run.

JASPAL: Yes.

VOICE: (*From cassette.*) It's that very feeling which keeps you like you are. You can change that fear into something good, something new. You can (*Spells out.*) F. E. A. R. Face Everything And Resolve. (*Pause.*) I can tell you're feeling kind of nervous, am I right? (*She nods.*) You know at the start sometimes you have to pretend, even if you don't feel it. You got to fake it. Remember sometimes you got to fake it to make it.

SATI has sat Ian Wright down on the shop stool. She does a sensual dance to him and again she mimes the words to the song 'Chura Liya.' Towards the end, she picks him up, they dance close again, this time much more sexually. By the end crescendo it is as though they have made love. She turns away from him shyly.

JASPAL's still listening to the tape.

See, it's not as hard as you thought is it? Now it's time for you to take responsibility. You know that important person from your past, you know who I mean.

JASPAL looks up and nods.

It's time to confront that person. (*Pause.*) That's a hard one isn't it. Why don't we have a practice first?

SATI gets up and walks away from Ian Wright. She then turns around and approaches him. She puts on a posh and seductive voice.

SATI: Hello my name's Sati and I live in… (*She shakes her head and says to herself.*) Too much like Blind Date. (*She starts again and approaches.*) I think we have so much to learn from the continentals don't you? The foreign players are so inventive and… No, no…he won't want to talk shop. (*She starts again and approaches.*) Do you think you might?… I mean have you ever…with an Indian girl…

JASPAL fixates on a wooden chair in front of the sofa. She looks at it confused.

VOICE: (*From cassette.*) My, you are getting brave aren't you. Now it's time to focus and concentrate. Forget about the outside world.

There is knocking at the shop door.

SATI: We're closed.

Knocking continues. She ignores it and it subsides. She takes a copy of '19' magazine and a large makeup box from behind the counter. She opens the magazine and goes to sit on a stool.

JASPAL is still fixating on the chair.

VOICE: (*From cassette.*) I know it may feel a little strange, but trust me its the first step.

JASPAL stares at the chair, she is obviously ill at ease.

How about saying Hi?

JASPAL: (*Slowly, addresses chair.*) Hello.

VOICE: (*From cassette.*) Come on.

JASPAL: Hello…Mum.

VOICE: (*From cassette. Frustrated.*) And.

JASPAL: (*Reluctantly.*) I want to make amends for the past.

VOICE: (*From cassette.*) Good. Now I want you to follow my instructions very closely.

SATI: (*Reads from magazine, in the same way as you would follow a recipe.*) First create your base by dotting foundation on your lids and around the eyes. Stroke it in gently. (*She rubs it in hard and looks at herself in her compact mirror. Frustrated.*) I can't see any difference (*She slaps more on. Reads again.*) Shade your lids with colour, blending with the fingertips. If you want to achieve a really dramatic effect you can combine as many as three contrasting shades. (*She appears a bit confused, looks up at Ian Wright cardboard cut-out which she has facing her. Brightens.*) I know. (*She delves into the make up box and takes two crayons. To Ian Wright cut-out while she is applying.*) You'll love this. Dramatic and original. (*She makes a pattern of red and white stripes on her eyes. As she finishes.*) What do you think?

No reply.

I hope you like it. I hope you like me. I want to be perfect for you.

JASPAL has moved closer to the chair.

VOICE: (*From cassette.*) Remember, it always helps to say it with love.

JASPAL: I didn't mean it. I didn't look after you. I know I should have. I'm sorry mum. (*She moves closer to the chair.*) Is it hurting? It's alright now, I'm here. It'll stop hurting now down there. I'm so sorry. For everything. Forgive me mum, will you do that? Will you? I need some kind of sign. Please Mummy.

The shop telephone starts to ring. SATI ignores it. It continues.

SATI: (*To phone.*) I told you, we're closed. (*Continues to apply make up.*)

JASPAL pleads with the chair.

JASPAL: Please. Talk to me. Talk to me.

SATI finishes – her make up is completed. As well as the red and white eye shadow, it is all over done and badly applied. The telephone is still ringing.

SATI: (*Annoyed.*) Right that's it.

She marches over to the telephone and picks it up.

Uncle I told you I'm on half… (*She stops and her expression changes to one of anxiety.*) …Oh… Hello. Yes it is. Speaking… But she can't be.

SATI stays on the phone. JASPAL's getting frustrated with the chair.

JASPAL: Well? (*Pause.*) What do you say?

SATI: Are you sure it's her? Is she alright? Can I talk to her?

JASPAL: (*She gets frustrated.*) I said what do you say.

SATI: No way. No I can't. (*Pause.*) Someone else will have to come. You don't understand. I have an important prior engagement.

JASPAL: For fuck's sake. (*She gets up and accidentally knocks over the chair. She stares for a moment and then it is as if whatever spell she has been under is broken.*) I can't fucking believe this. (*Horrified.*) Talking to a fucking chair. For fuck's sake. A fucking chair. (*She looks around.*)

SATI: Someone else will have to… Tell her I can't. You don't understand.

JASPAL: Someone's trying to fuck me up. (*Paces around, breathing deeply.*)

SATI puts the phone down and looks over at Ian Wright. Back to JASPAL.

VOICE: (*From cassette.*) Come on, surely after all this work you're not going to Fuck Everything and Run?

JASPAL: (*Gets herself together and kicks the chair.*) Shut the fuck up. She's got to be told.

Beat.

Patrick. (*She nods to herself.*) He'll know what to do.

Scene 11

1994 The Dole Office. FATHER and PATRICK are still waiting.
The number machine changes.

FATHER: (*Shouts.*) Please get some more staff here. (*To PATRICK.*) I can see them through there, (*Points.*) smoking and drinking.

PATRICK: Don't worry about it.

FATHER: I'm not worried. Why should I be worried?

SATI enters with BEJI. They both carry lots of Boots' bags, crammed with toiletries and make up. SATI drags along the Ian Wright cut-out. SATI's make up is by now dishevelled, she is still in her shalwar and JVC shirt. BEJI has her head covered and her head down. FATHER notices them.

What happened?

SATI goes over to him, and starts emptying contents of Boots bags on to his lap.

(*Looks at SATI.*) What… What are you doing?

SATI stops and looks at him hard.

SATI: (*Brightly/matter of fact.*) Hello dad. How are you?

FATHER: I am fine. What do you think you are doing?

SATI: Can you see me dad? Can you hear me? (*Picks up his hand, pulls it roughly to her cheek.*) Can you feel me?

FATHER: Why are you doing this…I…

SATI: (*Shouts, but still bright.*) Can you? Can you see, hear and feel me?

FATHER: Yes.

SATI: Good, Dad, that's good. Very good. You noticed… You noticed me. You noticed that I'm here.

FATHER: Why are you doing this? In front of all the unemployed people?

SATI: I don't give a shit about the unemployed.

FATHER: Have you gone mad?

SATI: It's not even your signing on day. Where's Mummy Two?

FATHER: I…I don't know. I think she took Raju for fencing lesson.

SATI: You've been here all the time haven't you.

FATHER: I need money.

SATI: Sitting here with your rubbishy pitiful poetry.

FATHER: It's not that bad.

SATI: (*Shouts.*) Yes it is!

FATHER: What…what happened?

SATI: (*Points to BEJI who is sitting on the floor, looking away.*) She's been shoplifting. Your mother has been stealing goods. Vitamin pills, hair accessories and over the counter medicines. They caught her dad, they caught her today, the Boots store detectives have had their eyes on her for months. They caught her and I had to deal with it because you were sitting here trying to finish your stupid poem.

FATHER: Beji?

SATI: I had somewhere to go, something to do, it was important. And I had to go and deal with it. (*Gestures to BEJI again.*) She pretended she couldn't speak English. She'd been swearing at the interpreter, reduced her to tears she did. I had to go Dad, I had to go and translate …It was horrible. I'm sixteen dad, I'm only sixteen…

BEJI: I'm sorry, I won't do it again, I promise.

FATHER: What happened?

SATI: She's been cautioned. They're not taking it any further.

FATHER: Thank God.

SATI: I had somewhere to go Dad. It was something. It meant something. And I missed it, you made me miss it.

FATHER: It's not my fault if she is a thief.

PATRICK: She's not a thief, she's just an old woman.

FATHER: What did you say?

PATRICK: She's not…

FATHER: How dare you. How dare you interfere in my family's business.

PATRICK: Jesus Christ.

FATHER: If I want to call my mother a thief, I will.

PATRICK: Fine.

FATHER: We are not like you people. In my community, we stick together and we look after each other.

PATRICK: Yeah, right.

FATHER: We show respect, we do not cause rumpus.

PATRICK: Of course not.

FATHER: Is this how you behave? Like a nosey parker. After everything I told you. I even read you my poem.

SATI: He doesn't mean any harm.

FATHER: So you take his side do you? Against your own father? Because he is like your Ian. Is that it? You like his people, better than you like me.

SATI: (*Holds cut-out protectively.*) Leave Ian Wright out of this.

FATHER: Is this what I deserve? In front of all the unemployed people? Am I such a bad father? Tell me. Am I such a bad father?

JASPAL enters.

JASPAL: Patrick.

She notices SATI, FATHER and BEJI. They all look at her in shock.

Oh shit. (*She laughs nervously.*) Oh God. Oh fuck. Shit.

SATI: Jaspal.

PATRICK: Let's go.

JASPAL: No. It's alright.

FATHER: I wish I could die now.

BEJI starts ranting like a chant and banging her head with her fist.

BEJI: What are the colours of God like? Oh God our kismet is so bad, oh God, our kismet is so bad.

FATHER: (*To PATRICK.*) Do you know my daughter? I should have known. Always the same with you people. Pimp or drug dealer, I should have known.

PATRICK: Here we go. Always the same old shit.

JASPAL: Shut up dad. Shut up with your racist shit.

FATHER: I am not a racist. Do not call me a racist. Is it true? Am I right? Is he your drug dealer?

JASPAL: Shut up. Drugs come from India anyway.

FATHER: Pakistan, not India. Don't bring India into this.

JASPAL: This is him, the black bastard I've been going out with. Who I've been living with, who I've been sleeping with, dad, who I've been having sex with…

FATHER: I am not listening.

JASPAL: Look at him Dad, look at him, he's black, he's my boyfriend and we…

FATHER: Don't call me dad. I am not your dad.

JASPAL: I feel sorry for you.

SATI: Jaspal, don't…

JASPAL: (*To SATI.*) Whose side are you on?

SATI: (*Sits rocking with cut-out, she is upset.*) Ian doesn't like fighting.

JASPAL: For fuck's sake.

SATI: Ian wants you to be more understanding.

FATHER: How can you understand this situation?

SATI: Ian says you have to make up.

PATRICK: Come on Sati, you need to get out of here.

FATHER: You leave her alone. One of my daughters is not enough for you?

PATRICK: She's upset you idiot.

JASPAL: Sati, you've got to stop. He's not real. He doesn't have feelings.

SATI: How do you know?

JASPAL: For fuck's sake. (*To FATHER.*) Are you going to stand by and let this go on?

FATHER: What can I do? You both think you are black.

JASPAL: She's going to turn into a nutter dad, you don't want her to end up…? Don't you care? Can't you see the signs. For fuck's sake.

FATHER: Sati is a good girl, you leave her alone.

JASPAL approaches SATI.

JASPAL: Sati, I'm trying to help. Ian can't hear you. Ian's made out of paper.

SATI: Stop it.

JASPAL: He's a cardboard fucking cut-out. He can't hear you.

SATI: Shut up. You're jealous of me. I know you are and I know you used to be a prostitute.

JASPAL: For fuck's sake. (*To FATHER.*) What did you say that for? He's not real. (*She moves closer to SATI.*)

SATI: And you hate us because mum never writes to you.

JASPAL: (*Screams and goes for the cut-out which she tears up.*) He's not real. He's just paper. He's not real.

SATI in turn screams and tries to salvage Ian Wright. There is a scuffle between them. JASPAL grabs hold of her and turns SATI round to face her.

JASPAL: (*To SATI.*) She's not in India.

FATHER: NO.

BEJI stops her chanting and gets up to confront JASPAL.

BEJI: Behsharam, kuthi, behsharam.

JASPAL ignores her and pushes her out of the way.

JASPAL: She didn't have a boy Sati. And he wasn't satisfied with two daughters, so he had to get a new wife.

FATHER: Don't listen.

JASPAL: After Mummy Two came you didn't like Mummy One did you dad? So you didn't mind when she went upstairs and locked herself away listening to her songs while she played with her sewing box.

BEJI: Behsharam.

JASPAL: I found her. She was trying to cut up her cunt with a pair of scissors.

FATHER: No.

JASPAL: She said there was a boy inside her and she was trying to get him out. I found her. Found her with all the blood.

FATHER: Stop it Jaspal. Please stop.

JASPAL: She's in a home five miles away, she won't come out now. She doesn't want to.

FATHER: Stop it. Don't listen. (*Points at JASPAL.*) It was her, she signed the papers. She sent her away.

JASPAL: It was only meant to be for a while. But after a bit she said she preferred it in there, at least she could play her music and sing her songs. I was going to tell you, Sati. But then, I couldn't, I didn't want to spoil it, not for you, not for you as well.

FATHER: It wasn't my fault. I wanted her to stay. But her, (*Points at JASPAL.*) she signed the form.

JASPAL: I had to. I didn't have any choice. Sati…

JASPAL goes to take SATI's hand. SATI backs away from her, in utter shock and disbelief, she looks around and runs out of the dole office. BEJI follows her.

BEJI: Sati, Sati, Sati. She tell lies. She is mad. Listen to me.

Number machine changes.

PATRICK: (*To FATHER.*) It's great the way you all stick together and look after each other.

PATRICK looks at his ticket and goes to sign on. FATHER and JASPAL sit motionless in the dole office seats. BEJI comes back inside. She approaches JASPAL.

BEJI: Now she is gone. Now you should be happy.

JASPAL: I'm on top of the world.

BEJI turns to the FATHER.

BEJI: You've left me with nothing. With no-one.

FATHER: I wanted us all to be together.

BEJI: Now in the days before I die. I must live in your hell.

FATHER: Please don't…

BEJI: In your hell with you. With nothing but your face to look at. Look at me…

FATHER: No, I…

BEJI: Look at me… (*She pulls his face to her face.*) Every time you look at me. I want you to remember.

FATHER: No…

BEJI: Remember what you did…you took everyone away from me…

FATHER: No, please Beji…

BEJI exits. The FATHER and JASPAL sit in silence.

Why Jaspal?

JASPAL: She needed to know. You can't tell lies forever

FATHER: She is a child. My child.

JASPAL: She's a girl, Dad. Not like Raju.

FATHER: I can't stand to look at you. Get out of my sight.

JASPAL: No. No. You made me like this. You sit and watch me.

FATHER: You made yourself Jaspal, into this…behsharam…

JASPAL: I'm my father's daughter.

FATHER: And now you want Sati to share your shame.

JASPAL: You fucking hypocrite.

FATHER: She is a good girl, she is clean. I wanted to keep her away from this.

JASPAL: She's my sister. We've got the same blood. You do remember our mother don't you?

Pause.

FATHER: Do you hate me so much?

JASPAL: I don't hate you dad. I feel sorry for you.

FATHER: Your pity is worse than your hate.

JASPAL: I feel sorry for all of us.

FATHER: So much trouble, there has been so much trouble.

JASPAL: I know.

FATHER: So many bad things have happened.

JASPAL: Yes dad.

FATHER: But it was not my fault.

JASPAL: Like I said, you can't tell lies forever.

JASPAL gets up to go.

FATHER: Jaspal…shall I still bring you saag?

JASPAL: No dad. No thanks. I can make my own from now on. (*She goes to leave and looks back.*) Why did you bring it? Every week. You must have thought of me in some way.

FATHER: After all the shame you brought to us. I had enough. I didn't want any more.

JASPAL: What do you mean?

FATHER: I brought you food so I would never have to see you begging. So I would not have to see any more of your shame.

JASPAL stops for a moment, then continues on her way out.

JASPAL: There's always Raju dad. You've got a son. Now there's something to be proud of.

She exits. FATHER sits alone on stage.

FATHER: I can't…I can't face looking at him. (*He looks to where JASPAL has gone. He breaks down.*) I feel shame. So much shame. I want my girls. Where are my girls? I want my girls. (*He looks around and slowly gathers himself together. He opens his book. He takes out his pen. Recites as before.*) Tu meri zindagi meh ay…

Scene 12

1998. The Dressing Room. JASPAL sits, SATI stands. Silence.

JASPAL: I'm sorry.

SATI: I understand.

JASPAL: I thought it was for your own good.

SATI: It's alright. I understand now.

JASPAL: I waited for you.

SATI: I know.

SATI takes JASPAL's hands in hers.

JASPAL: I wanted you to come.

SATI: I wanted to.

JASPAL: I waited and waited.

SATI: I was angry. I didn't understand.

JASPAL: I'm clean now.

SATI: I can see.

JASPAL: Really clean.

SATI: Have you ever been to see Mum?

JASPAL: Not for a long time. I used to go. Every week. Not any more.

SATI: We've got each other.

JASPAL: Yes.

SATI: I'm your family now. You've got me.

JASPAL: What about the others?

SATI: Mummy Two left. She took Raju on a Mediterranean cruise.

JASPAL: So her and Dad…?

SATI: She sends pictures. Raju's ten now. She enters him for ballroom dancing competitions, he's won loads of medals.

JASPAL: What about dad?

SATI: The same. And Beji. Both still waiting for Uncle Comrade… What happened to Patrick?

JASPAL: He helped me to get Kiran going. But then he went. He couldn't stand me at the end. I don't blame him.

SATI: I'm sorry.

JASPAL: Don't be. I'm not. Anyway I'm glad you came.

SATI: So am I… Jaspal I need a fag.

JASPAL: You're weak that's what you are.

SATI: Please.

JASPAL: Go on then. I was weak once.

SATI lights up.

SATI: You know. I've been thinking a lot about Mummy One, I mean mum.

JASPAL: Oh yeah.

SATI: I've been to visit her. I mean she won't leave or anything. I've been on at her but she won't. But she's doing ever so well. I was thinking, we should go and visit her together.

JASPAL is still and has her back to SATI and the audience.

What do you say?

Silence.

Well?

JASPAL: What do you want?

SATI: Nothing, I thought would be nice for her, I'm sure she'd like to see us.

JASPAL turns to face SATI.

JASPAL: You've missed your chance.

SATI: What?

JASPAL: She's dead Sati, Mum's dead.

SATI: No...no she's not.

JASPAL: She died two years ago of a bleeding heart attack.

SATI: She can't have.

JASPAL: I've got her ashes at home in a jam jar.

SATI: What?

JASPAL: I couldn't decide what to do with her, so I thought I'd keep her. Keep her with me.

SATI: No.

JASPAL: Oh yes. You little liar. (*She laughs.*) What have you really come for?

SATI: I wanted to see her... (*She starts to cry.*) ...I wanted my mum...I want my mum.

JASPAL: I'll lend you the jar if you like.

SATI: Please Jaspal. Stop it.

JASPAL: Come on. We've done enough Happy Families for one day don't you think?

SATI: I wanted to do something right.

JASPAL: So you thought you'd lie?

SATI: You did.

JASPAL: So fucking what? We're even now. Is that what this is about?

SATI: I was frightened. I thought I might end up like her. Like Mummy One. It was after I met him

JASPAL: Who?

SATI: Ian Wright. At this party. It brought it all back.

JASPAL: What?

SATI: It made me remember the way I felt before. When I had him with me. I kept trying to get close to him to tell him but I couldn't get past the bodyguard. I only wanted to talk. Just for a minute. Like I used to. All those times, all the things I used to tell him about. I tried to get near him, but they wouldn't let me through. I had too much to drink. And I was sick in the toilets and I cried. I cried and cried. I thought about Mummy One, about when she hurt herself and I wanted to copy her. I wanted to make myself bleed like her. And so I did. I made a right old mess. Doing the same damage as she did.

JASPAL: You silly cow.

SATI: Afterwards I got scared. Scared of myself. So I decided I should go and see her. I thought it might help me. And I thought you'd help me find her.

JASPAL: You're too late.

SATI: I know.

JASPAL: You missed your chance.

SATI: Yes. Not like you. Seems like you did the right thing after all.

JASPAL: I suppose.

SATI moves towards JASPAL. Their reflections can be seen in all three mirrors of the dressing table.

SATI: You're my sister.

JASPAL: So?

SATI: We're the same. Same blood. Same badness. As bad as each other.

At this point, both their reflections can be seen in all three mirrors, gradually their reflection overlap and it is hard to make one out from the other.

Do you see now?

JASPAL: Yeah. It's the same old damage. Right pair of cunts aren't we? Who would have thought it?

SATI: What?

JASPAL: You. You turned out as bad as me. Worse by the looks of you.

SATI: I'm sorry Jaspal. I won't come here again.

COMPERE: (*Off.*) Kiran, Jerry wants to know if you're going to do 'Ticket to Ride'.

JASPAL: (*Shouts.*) Tell him no. And tell him to get the key right. It's C flat.

COMPERE: (*Off.*) What love?

JASPAL: (*Shouts.*) C fucking flat. (*To SATI.*) Honestly some of these people. Talented as shit.

JASPAL gets up to go out. As she passes SATI she takes her in her arms and kisses her hard on the lips.

SATI: What?

JASPAL: You're my fucking sister aren't you? Come on.

Scene 13

1998. Red velvet curtains are behind a small raised platform on top of which there is an empty microphone.

COMPERE: (*Off.*) And now ladies and gents, it's time to lock up your sons. Here she is, back from the dead, our very own Kiran Carpenter.

The sound of applause again (as at beginning.). JASPAL comes out, all dolled up.

JASPAL: Thankyou, thank you all so much. Special thanks to my band the wonderful Asian Invasion. I'm going to leave you with one of my favourites and I'd like to dedicate this one to my sister who came to see the show tonight.

Music starts. JASPAL does a stupendous version of 'Only Yesterday'. She leaves the stage to uproarious applause. Curtains close.

The End